The Unspeakable Gift

The Unspeakable Gift

A Testimony of Deliverance from the New Age Movement.

by Mary Ellis

The Unspeakable Gift

by Mary Ellis

Cover Design by Tim Agnew

All Scripture quotations in this book are from the King James Version of the Bible unless otherwise identified.

Printed in United States of America

Printed by

Library of Congress Cataloging-in-Publication Data

Ellis, Mary.
The unspeakable gift / by Mary Ellis.
p. cm.
ISBN 1-56722-015-0 :
1. Ellis, Mary. 2. Converts, Pentecostal--Texas--Pearland--Biography.
3. Pearland (Tex.)--Religion--20th century. 4. Texas-Religion--20th century.
5. Oneness doctrine (Pentecostalism)
I. Title.
BX8763.Z8E55 1993
289.9′4--dc20
[B] 93-31506
CIP

Where Is Life?

Is it in cycles, like spring and fall?
Or perhaps, as some think, a little in all?

Poor are they who think they've found
Truth in nothing but ashes in the ground.
Some say it's in the almighty "BE,"
But I know, my Lord, that life is in Thee!

For all else is death beside the exuberance of
The power of life found in the Dove,
Who promises joy and peace beyond measure,
And delivers an exceedingly abundant treasure!

No, I am not ashamed of the gospel of the Cross,
For without it, I count my life but a loss.

Phyllis Buckner

Contents

Foreword *9*
Acknowledgments *11*
1. Strike One *13*
2. Trying Again *23*
3. Strike Two *35*
4. Strike Three? *43*
5. Mardel *55*
6. The Living Word *67*
7. Turning Point *79*
8. A Place to Worship *91*
9. Answers *101*
10. Storming the Gates of Hell *115*
11. The Impossible *123*
12. The Doctors *135*
13. Beauty and the Beast *147*
14. Helen *161*
15. The Presence *173*
16. The Full Gospel *181*
17. Water and Spirit *195*
18. Bob *209*
19. Miracles *219*

Foreword

In *The Unspeakable Gift,* Mary Ellis describes her family's stirring pilgrimage from traditional religion into truth. Since coming to the Lord, she and her husband, Bob, have grown into a modern-day Aquila and Priscilla. This couple has won and discipled many souls to the Lord and has been a constant source of comfort and encouragement to me.

Bob, like Aquila, is both a nurturer and a developer. On many occasions, I have watched him help others in distress with his characteristic patience and concern. Mary, like Priscilla, often takes the lead in explaining the Scriptures to many an Apollos. Energetic, sincere, and humorous, she is persistent in showing others the truth.

Their story is typical of many others coming to the Lord in this day when spiritual hunger is often disguised by success and other things, when prior marriages and the children involved remain a continuous challenge, and when incremental victories keep people trying. This book, at the very least, will give all believers a greater understanding and appreciation of people seeking to escape the world's grasp.

Mary wrote this book with much encouragement from me and others. We feel that the Ellis family's story can aid others in their quest for truth. In addition to endorsing this book, I can wholeheartedly recommend its author, her husband, her family, and her God. So, find a comfortable chair and a box of tissues and share in Mary's touching story of her search and discovery of *The Unspeakable Gift.*

Ken Gurley, Pastor
Pearland Tabernacle

Acknowledgments

Special thanks to

Pastor Ken Gurley for his godly life that allows me to trust his godly counsel;

Phyllis Buckner, my sister, for her poetic works that so beautifully blended with this testimony of God's saving power and grace; and

Lisa Cropper for assisting me with her grammatical expertise.

Chapter One

Strike One

"Jennifer, I never planned on divorce. It wasn't part of my vocabulary. The thought has tormented me for two and one-half years. I've asked myself a hundred questions, but I still don't have any answers. I never dreamed life could be so tough."

A tear fell on Jennifer as I looked down at her innocent face surrounded with blond ringlets. She had the light-colored hair of her father. "I'll take care of you, Jennifer. You don't have to worry," I quickly explained to her as if at eighteen months of age she could understand my thoughts and sentences. "Your daddy can see you whenever he wants to, Jen. I'll never stop him from seeing you. He's your daddy." She was sound asleep now. I touched her soft little cheek, rearranged the tiny blanket, and tiptoed away from the crib.

My body was thin and bony. The gnawing pain in my stomach would not allow much food. I walked into the living room of the small apartment. My possessions were meager and had not taken long to move. The sunburst clock purchased with green stamps was mounted over the dinette. One of Mom's oil paintings colored the wall above the sofa. Everything was in place. A realization of stillness pervaded my thoughts, and suddenly I became lonely.

What now? I wondered to myself. I'm only twenty-one. I'm too young to stay single the rest of my life. The knot in my stomach tightened at the beginning of this new mental struggle.

Years of childhood teaching against divorce came to regimental attention forming a wall against these new thoughts. "Divorce is wrong; remarriage is out of the question," came the sharp voice from that intricate brain function called memory.

"What did those teachers know?" I countered. "They couldn't possibly understand my situation. They were old people, probably in their forties or something. They had fine husbands, fine homes, and fine marriages. Who could be cruel enough to condemn a twenty-one-year-old to a life of isolation?" This new barrage of thoughts shot back at the regiment of precepts. The wall of memories suffered considerable damage that night.

The parking-lot lights filtered through the curtained window. Peeking out, I looked at the empty balconies and then down to the cars below. Even if someone had been outside, I did not know any of my new neighbors yet.

Suddenly I decided to talk to God. That was a new idea. Although I had been a regular churchgoer for nineteen of my twenty-one years, I only knew the rote prayers of my denomination. It had never occurred to me before then to just talk to God with my own words. I had never felt the need before.

The dull red carpet was somewhat worn and had a thin pad underneath. I only knew one position in which to pray and that was on my knees. I knelt in silence for a moment, trying to figure out how to converse with a God I could not see. "Will He hear me? Does He care that my insides hurt? What does *He* think about my current status in life?" I asked myself.

"God," I began gingerly, "these past two and one-half years have been nothing but pain. I don't understand, God. I didn't know You would let a person hurt so much. I've gone to church and prayed all of my life. Where are You now, God? I'm scared and confused. Amen."

Rising to my feet, I knew I had to get some sleep. Five o'clock in the morning would arrive and demand a day of work. With a deep sense of responsibility, I would not allow myself to miss a day of work or be late.

Jennifer has been a morning person from Day One. We shared the one bedroom of the apartment, and when I opened my eyes she was standing in the crib grinning at me. I smiled back. "I'm glad I have you to share my life with, Jennifer."

I chattered endlessly while feeding and dressing her. "Someday, Jennifer, maybe I can stay home and take care of you. Right now I must go to work and leave you at day care. I'll come back and get you as fast as I can, okay?" The spoon banging and food splattering assured me that her baby world held no comprehension of adult turmoil.

The mortgage company where I worked completely filled the building near one of Houston's many freeways. The front office was a huge room with row upon row of desks. I dug into the trays on top of my desk, but it was difficult to think about forms and paper work. After several hours of determined effort, I saw Linda walk toward me and motion for the coffee room. I was ready for a break. "Come on, Margaret," I urged the other young woman nearby.

We had our choice of tables in the empty break room and could talk freely. Margaret wanted a baby, but she and her husband were unsuccessful in having a child of their own. She gave us an update on the medical testing they were undergoing. We looked at the top of her naturally blond head as she dipped rosy cheeks downward and shared her feelings of embarrassment at the extensive testing. "It's worth it," she said quietly, "if it will help us have a child of our own."

Pictures of Jennifer's antics came to my mind. "It will be worth it," I reassured her.

Linda, the spunky one of the group, blurted out, "I'll be glad if I even get a husband."

"You're hardly an old maid," Margaret and I chimed almost simultaneously.

Linda proceeded to tell us her dating woes, but sprinkled throughout her conversation were words I mentally assigned to men and especially sailors. Margaret's cheeks blushed a deeper color and down went that blond head again. I felt inquisitive instead of shy, however. "Linda, how can you talk like that?" I asked, looking at her.

My world had been sheltered, because I had married right after high school. I was, therefore, a naive young woman even as a divorced person.

"Mary, don't you know that words are not right or wrong? They are only to express feelings," Linda answered in her woman-of-the-world voice.

With that new thought planted in my mind, it was time to go back to work.

That evening, I climbed the stairs with Jennifer grasping one hand and a grocery bag balanced on my hip. "Up we go," I said in a singing voice to Jennifer as I gently pulled and lifted her up each step.

"Better look where you're going," I heard from a deep voice at the top of the stairs.

Looking up, I saw a young, dark-haired man standing near my door. He was small framed and had a day's stubble of a beard on his face. Grinning widely he said, "Hi! My name's Ron. I live right below you and came up to meet you."

"Hi," I responded with friendly ease. Not being an initiator, I was glad a neighbor made the first move toward friendship. Ron took the groceries from my arm while I unlocked my door.

Standing at the door, Ron continued talking with me until I said, "Hey, look, I'm about to fix a meal for myself and Jennifer. Won't you join us?"

How could anyone, at the age of twenty-one, having once been married, be so ignorant of relationships with the male gender? Little did I realize that my extension of hospitality was opening a door to a road of shallow encounters.

I was glad to be neighborly to Ron, and he filled my otherwise lonely evenings with companionship, but before many days passed, Ron was making advances to me. I managed to talk my way out of close circumstances for the first few weeks. Then I began listening to his reasoning.

"Mary, it's okay for two people who care about each

other to be close,'' he chided.

''We can just be friends, Ron. Intimacy is for marriage,'' I said weakly. My own thoughts were confused and full of questions. After all, I had never believed in divorce, but my marriage had ended.

''Marriage is only a piece of paper. What really counts is what two people have together,'' Ron replied with skill.

His reasoning filled the potholes in my thinking. Years later I would gain an understanding of the powers of darkness that were making entrance into my life that night.

Through Ron I met others at the apartment complex. There was another divorced woman named Thelma who lived across the courtyard. She had three small children to care for, and she loved to cook. Her lackadaisical personality was calming to my frayed nerves, and we became fast friends. We encouraged each other, and each of us would readily babysit for the other.

On some evenings Thelma would cook and invite me and Ron over to eat. On other evenings I would do the cooking and Thelma would bring her children and join me, Jennifer, and Ron. The lonely life I had envisioned did not exist. Our group grew as a few other singles began to join in our capricious lifestyle.

There was plenty of activity among us in the apartment complex. I would barely get home from work before my friends would come over. ''Hey everybody, give me enough time to change clothes,'' I pleaded.

I turned on the stereo and went to the bedroom to put on faded jeans and a T-shirt. Combing my natural curly hair was next to impossible. I ran my fingers through the long, dark curls to disentangle them. When I came back out, my friendly neighbors were comfortably seated and lounging in the living room listening to the music. "What's that odd smell?" I asked.

"It's grass. Here, have a toke," Ron offered.

"No, thanks," I said quickly.

"Hey, it's all right. We're just having fun," said another neighbor.

"That's okay," I said. "I just don't do that."

Linda drew on the rolled paper and asked, "Have you ever tried it?"

"No, I don't want to."

"What's wrong with it?" Ron asked in a derisive tone. "We're not out getting drunk. We're sitting around laughing and listening to music. Now what crime is that?"

I looked around the room. My youthful mind did not stop to consider that illegality was enough to make marijuana wrong. Everyone was smiling and relaxing. It looked so innocent. The perspectives of my friends were making inroads in my thinking. Right and wrong were not black and white. Reasons for every action validated gratification. "Well, okay. I'll try it," I answered haltingly.

Another dark door was opened in my life. I fit in with my new friends. It was a life of nighttime and drugs. The words I had relegated to men and sailors were becoming familiar to my hearing. It wasn't long before they entered my vocabulary. After all, hadn't Linda said that words were neither right nor wrong? I consoled myself.

One night as several of us were eating and talking and laughing, there was a knock on my door. I opened the door and there stood a tall, dark, handsome young man. He had a head full of short, black, curly hair and big brown eyes. There was no grin from this guy nor the easygoing greeting of "hi" spoken among my friends.

Flashing dark eyes above a deliberate smile peered down at me and a sophisticated "hello" rolled smoothly from his mouth.

"H-Hello," I stammered back.

"I'm Mike," he said with the quiet tones that come with confidence. "I just moved in a few days ago and would like to meet you and your friends here."

"Well, come in, Mike. I'm Mary and this is Ron, Thelma, and Richard. They live here too. This is Linda. She and I work together."

The rest of the evening was subdued. Everyone was aware of the presence of our new acquaintance. Eventually, my friends began to leave until finally I sat there with Ron and Mike.

"You're beautiful," Mike said, looking past Ron to me. He was looking at me as if Ron didn't exist.

Ron made a few attempts to verbally defend what he thought was his territory. The problem was that Ron's own concepts had torn down fences in my mind. Without understanding how it happened, I had become open game and still did not know I was no more than a pawn to these men.

Ron must have been waiting for me to usher Mike to the door. If Ron had taken the time to really know me, he would have seen my unassertive ways and my fear of offending people. I certainly was no match for this man who so easily and quickly intruded into my life. Ron made his exit.

Mike and I were together for several months, but I was only one of a string of girls for him. Then I met Nicki. At thirty-three, Nicki was an older man to me. He knew how to focus on a person. Nicki would look straight into my eyes when he spoke or when he was listening to me. He swept me away from Mike by going beyond the conversational sentiments of "you're beautiful." Nicki would discuss feelings and subjects that held my interest and even caused me to branch out in reading and learning. Often, he would find me snuggled into a chair reading a volume from his set of literary classics, and then I would excitedly relate what I had been reading to him. His rapt attention made me feel that I was really important to someone.

For almost a year Nicki had me convinced of his devotion to me. One Saturday afternoon in July, I went to Nicki's apartment unannounced. When I knocked on the door, there was no answer. I walked out to the pool. Holding my hand up to shade my eyes from the sunlight, I scanned the sun soakers looking for Nicki. "There he is," I muttered when I spotted him.

"Nicki!" I called.

He turned and looked in my direction. "Hi!" he yelled, waving at me.

Then he turned back and spoke to a pretty, dark-haired woman nearby. The two of them came over to me. "This is Sherry," Nicki said without a trace of guilt, fear, or remorse.

I looked first at Sherry then at Nicki. Maybe it's his sister or something, I thought.

"Hello, Sherry," I said extending my hand.

"Hello," she said in return.

Nicki put his arm around Sherry's shoulder. "This is my new friend," he explained.

"Oh. I see. Uh . . . well, uh . . . I'm very glad to meet you." The words were choking in my throat.

Nicki was telling me how he had met Sherry, but I couldn't hear all of his words. I looked at Sherry again. She's pretty, I thought to myself. She doesn't know; she has no idea that I have been Nicki's girlfriend for almost a year. How can he do this to me? How can he stand here so glibly and introduce a new girlfriend as if I were a piece of junk to be tossed aside? Didn't this past year mean anything to him?

I had stopped breathing. When I realized it, I took in a deep breath and said, "Well, I have to go now. I'll see you later, Nicki."

Not knowing what to do with Sherry, I managed to force out the words, "Nice to have met you, Sherry." Turning away my face, I left quickly before the tears began to fall.

I retreated with terrible emotional wounds. To Ron and Mike I may have been no more than another trophy on a shelf, but Nicki deceived me into thinking he really cared about me and even loved me. The latter was a hurt that would not heal quickly.

I kept to myself, trying to figure things out. My life had spun out of control. Again, I was glad to have Jennifer. She was always there for me to take care of her needs. Jennifer brought an aspect of stability to my topsy-turvy life.

Chapter Two

Trying Again

Driving down Interstate 45 with Jennifer strapped in safely beside me, I was carrying on a mostly one-sided conversation. Once in a while Jennifer would interject her addition to the dialogue in her three-year-old language.

The sound of a horn honking turned my head toward the lane next to me. There was a nice-looking fellow waving my direction. I quickly faced forward again, not wanting to be the object of girl watching. Suddenly a file from my memory banks leaped forward and I took another look to my left. That *is* Mark, came the declaration in my mind. How can this be? How can you meet someone you dated six years ago in high school while you are traveling at fifty-five miles per hour on a freeway? What's he doing pulling in front of me? Oh, he wants me to pull off to the shoulder.

I stopped my car behind Mark's. He jumped out and came to my window.

"Mark, what are you doing? How did you see me on that busy freeway? What's going on? Are you married? Do you still live around here? How are you?" I quizzed him in rapid-fire fashion as if one meeting could catch up on six years of information.

Looking at Jennifer sitting next to me Mark said, "I guess you're married, huh?"

"No, I'm divorced," I answered without fear to this old friend of mine.

Mark informed me that he was in the army and was home on furlough. We made plans for a date and rejoined the moving traffic.

He still looks the same, I thought as I drove along the freeway. Mark was of medium height for a man, but his five-foot-ten-inch frame housed a powerful build. His black hair was kept short and neat. True, he was in the army, but Mark had always been clean-cut and fastidious.

I envisioned the bygone days of high school. Mark and I had been in the same geometry class. Mark's desk was at the front of the row next to mine. I was in the last desk of my row. With my elbows propped on my desk, I held my chin in my hands and stared at Mark while I daydreamed through class. My no-sweat, honor-roll grades suffered when I failed geometry. It was the only subject I ever failed in my life.

During the course of Mark's furlough, we dated and caught up on the events of each other's life. Our dating halted when I became ill. At first I didn't realize I was sick. I was sitting at my desk at the office and dropped my pencil. I picked it up from the floor and went back to the paper work. A few minutes later I dropped the pencil again.

Pat, an older woman whose desk was not too far from mine, asked, "Mary, what's wrong with you today?"

"I'm fine. I just dropped my pencil," I told her with all honesty.

I went back to my paper work, but I was aware that Pat was watching me. With careful concentration, I completed the forms on my desk and then reached for more with my left hand. The pencil in my right hand fell to the floor again.

What's happening to me? I wondered silently. I leaned over to pick up the pencil, but this time coming back up was difficult. My head felt like a fog had settled in. "Oh, I'm so tired. I didn't notice it before."

Pat came over to my desk. "You look kind of pale. Why don't you go home and get some rest?"

"No. I'll be okay. I don't like to miss work. I have to take care of myself and Jennifer."

It was difficult to get through the rest of the day, but I made it. I picked up Jennifer from the day care and went straight home to my apartment. I was lying on the couch resting when Mark came over.

"Hi, Mark. Have you had supper yet?"

"Yeah, I have. I just wanted to see you."

As we sat and talked, I kept scratching my legs and arms. Mark noticed my incessant itching. "Did you get into some ants or something?"

"No. I don't know what it is. There aren't any marks on my skin. I just itch. Look, I'm getting bruised from scratching. What do you think it could be?"

"I can't see anything either," he said upon close inspection of my arm.

We didn't think much more about it. I tried rubbing

lotion on my skin for several days and continued going to work. It was the itching that sent me to the doctor.

"Hepatitis? What's that?" I asked the doctor.

"It's a disease that affects your liver," he explained.

"How did I get it?"

"I'm not sure that you have it yet," said the doctor. "My nurse will call you tomorrow with the test results."

A phone was ringing in the distance. It rang and rang and rang and rang. The sound was getting louder. Oh, that's *my* phone, I suddenly realized.

I got up from the bed to answer the phone. The room started spinning and I grabbed the table by the bed. My sister, Phyllis, had spent the night at my apartment. Where's Phyllis? I wondered. Where's Jennifer? What time is it?

No one was there to answer my questions. The phone was ringing. I tried to walk toward the sound, but I felt as if I were walking through water. "I'm coming. I'm coming," I called out as if the phone could transfer my message to the caller.

"Hello."

"Mary, this is the nurse. We've been trying to reach you all day. Your test came back positive. You have hepatitis. The doctor wants you to come in for a gamma globulin injection. Tell your close family and friends to come in for one also. You will have to stay in bed for at least three or four weeks. The doctor will talk to you when you come in."

"Thank you," I stammered with ebbing strength. My eyes located the clock. It was two-thirty in the afternoon.

"Where's Jennifer?" I anxiously asked out loud after I hung up the phone.

The phone rang again immediately. "Hello. Oh, hi, Mom."

My mother sounded concerned. "I've been trying to call you all day. Your office didn't hear from you. Phyllis called me from her office and said she took Jennifer to day care this morning because you were sleeping so soundly. I was getting worried about you."

"I just got a call from the doctor's office. They said that I have hepatitis. Jennifer and I will have to get shots. Phyllis will need one too. I will have to stay in bed, Mom. How will I keep my job?"

"Hepatitis! Where did you get that?"

"I don't know. I don't even know what it is yet. The nurse said I have to go to bed. What am I going to do?"

"We will get you moved in with me, Mary. You will need help with Jennifer."

My mom was a widow and lived by herself. She brought me to her apartment and put me to bed. My sisters and Mark emptied my apartment and put my things in storage, bringing only clothing and small items to my mother's place. Mom took Jennifer to day care and went to her own job during the daytime.

"Guess what I found out today?" my mother asked as she brought Jennifer in with her.

Before I could ask what it was, she was already offering the information. "When I picked up Jennifer this afternoon, I heard a day care worker talking to a parent. It seems that a couple of workers at the day care have come down with hepatitis. Other parents have come down with it too. Now we know where you got it."

During the month that I spent in bed, Mark came to visit me frequently. His furlough ended and he came to say goodbye.

Mark leaned close to the bed and touched my hair. "I wish I didn't have to go, Mary."

"I know, Mark. I've gotten to know you all over again and now you have to leave."

"What will happen to you and Jennifer?"

"We'll be all right. I'll be back on my feet in no time. I'm used to taking care of us. Mom will help me until I'm well."

"Mary, will you marry me?"

I looked at Mark to see if he was serious. He had caught me by surprise.

"Don't answer me now," he said. "Think about it and I will call you next week."

He leaned forward to kiss me. "Don't get close, Mark! You'll catch it!"

He leaned back his head and laughed.

"What are you laughing at? I'm serious. I don't want you to get hepatitis." Then I said more quietly, "I like to hear you laugh. You have a deep, rich laugh." Lightening up again, I gave him a playful push and firmly stated, "Here, you can kiss this cheek. I'll turn my head and not breathe any germs on you."

Mark kissed my cheek and rose to leave. "I'll call you next week. I hope you'll say yes. I want to take care of you and Jennifer."

Those were magic words. Mark left, and I told Mom about his proposal.

I spent the next several days wondering what to do. I felt comfortable with Mark because he was from the past. I was afraid of another relationship with someone I didn't know very well. Mark seemed to be a responsible person, and besides that, he was proposing marriage and not just a casual relationship. That settled it; I would marry him.

We were married by a justice of the peace. The ceremony was barely over when I noticed a change in Mark. It was as if the prey was captured and the interest in the hunt was over.

Mark was a wonderful stepfather to Jennifer. He was loving but firm with her. I marveled at his parenting capabilities. Jennifer's short life had been jostled by my chaos, and Mark was exactly what she needed.

Mark was not as good of a husband as he was a stepfather. He had very little to do with me after we married. This marriage had to work as far as I was concerned. Never wanting one divorce, I definitely had no intentions of two.

The remainder of Mark's stint in the army provided a rationale for his frequent absences during the first six months of our marriage. But when he rejoined civilian life, my hopes of his attention were dashed as he continued to live within his own interests.

I read a book about being a wonderful wife, one that a husband couldn't resist. One of the instructions was to be involved in things that interested him. When Mark was building his dune buggy to race, I was right there asking what I could do. I sanded rusty ends of metal tubing and was the official tool "gofer."

When the races rolled around, I packed up Jennifer with water jugs and sun hats, and off we went to watch the races. The tracks were in big, open fields with muddy ruts, a lot of sun, little or no breeze, and no shade trees. In my estimation, these races were not fun, but I sure wasn't going to show it.

Mark drove the truck onto the field. Jennifer and I climbed down to the grass watching carefully for cocklebsurs, potholes, and ant hills. Jennifer took a few tentative steps, then screamed and ran to grab hold of my knees. "It was only a butterfly, Jennifer. You're okay. It was pretty. Did you see the colors on its wings?"

"I don't like budderflies, Mommy. They scare me," she cried while still clinging to me.

Jennifer frightened easily. Insects and the crunching of leaves under her feet would send her scurrying to look for protection. "I know what you feel like, Jennifer. I look for security too," I said quietly. I was speaking more to myself than to Jennifer, who wouldn't even know the meaning of the word *security*.

I pulled out lawn chairs from the back of the truck. Setting Jennifer's little chair next to mine for later, I pulled her up to my lap and snuggled with her. "It'll be okay, Jen. Let's watch the races."

It would be a while before there was a race to watch. The men were taking their homemade dune buggies from their trailers. They congregated near the track talking and making mechanical checks. Other wives were on the field in twos or in small groups. They looked like longtime friends. Being too shy to introduce myself to them, I huddled Jennifer closer to me singing little songs and talking to her.

The morning seemed endless. I wondered why it took the men so long to get ready for a race. Why couldn't they just get in and go? Mark stayed with the men and I was lonely. "Let's go to the truck and get our snack, Jen."

I gave Jennifer half of a peanut butter sandwich and

a cup of Kool-Aid. The other half of the sandwich was plenty for me; my stomach was squeezed into a knot.

Jennifer's fears were subsiding and she was ready to play. We tossed a Frisbee back and forth until she began to look tired. Then the roar of engines caught our attention.

"Look, Jennifer! They're ready for the race. Let's go watch." I tried to sound excited to her. I knew how fast they made the laps, and then we would be waiting again.

Jennifer jumped up and down and clapped her hands as she looked toward the speeding dune buggies flinging mud into the air. I strained to keep my eyes on Mark although it was difficult to tell one buggy from the other. They were approaching the turn and moving fast. One driver was out in front. The next three were neck to neck, and two more were pressing from behind trying to catch up.

The three close cars reached the curve. One of them spun around. "Aw, fell over," said Jennifer.

My eyes were closed in case he crashed into the other cars; I didn't want to see it. Hearing only the roaring engines, I reopened my eyes and looked for Mark. Buggies and drivers were covered with mud. There was no way to tell who was who. I sat back down in the lawn chair. The race was over. It was time to wait again.

Jennifer looked sleepy. There was a quilt in the truck, so I got it and spread it on the ground for her. She had been out in the sun all morning and easily fell asleep. I pulled out a book to read. The loneliness was quelled as I immersed myself into the book.

The marriage that I had hoped would soothe my previous emotional wounds only cut into them deeper. Somehow I had lost track of that singular experience of talking to God. Instead I had been distracted into searching for answers to life's pain: searching for peace, love, and happiness.

I had a husband, provision, and a child, but there was a terrible empty feeling deep inside of me. I could not explain it and had no idea why other people seemed to go so easily through life. Something in me felt driven and compelled to find answers.

Attempting to fill this inner void, I became an avid reader, drawn to books with spiritual content. Because of my complete ignorance of God's Word, having never opened or even owned a Bible in my life, I had no discernment between truth and error. Blindly I began filling my mind with error.

I read about a man who went into a self-hypnotic trance and was able to pinpoint other people's physical problems and then give them solutions. The man had a very high percentage rate of accuracy. This same man, when in a trance, would describe past lives of people. He would describe details about places in the world where he had never been. Researchers would then study this information and again find amazing accuracy.

In the back of these books was the address of a nationwide organization whose members studied the concepts described through this man's trances. I was fascinated. Writing to the headquarters, I received a reply telling me where a group was meeting in my area. Having read books about this organization and the people behind it, I had a common bond with the group I wanted to meet, enabling me to push past shyness and make the phone call.

We met in the home of a woman named Janie. Belonging to this group opened up a new circle of friends to me. It also provided a mental outlet to retreat from my current marriage problems. Determined to make this second marriage work, I had found a means of emotional survival.

Chapter Three

Strike Two

On Tuesday evening I arrived at Janie's house with Jennifer in tow. I was the only one with a child that small, and everyone in the group loved her. Our meeting lasted about two hours, so I tucked Jennifer in to sleep on a couch nearby.

Our group was just about assembled when a new member arrived. He was a tall man in jeans and motorcycle boots who introduced himself as Bob. His hair was dark but thinning on top, and he had a friendly smile. I never dreamed at that moment that I had just met my third husband.

Although we met at Janie's house, group members took turns leading the sessions. The format was always the same, and the leader for the week, Jerry, opened the meeting with a very short prayer. Prayers among this group consisted of short affirmations or quoting the Lord's Prayer, which was familiar to everyone.

The group leader was responsible for keeping the

discussion moving and to ensure that all members had an opportunity to express themselves. These people were trained in group dynamics through books supplied by the headquarter's office. The meetings were well organized and kept to a time schedule. These attributes developed successful meetings, and this type of gathering proliferated around the country.

Thousands of people regularly attended similar meetings, searching for answers to their pain and troubles. I was one of them. Missing a meeting was out of the question. I was drawn to it, pulled to it; my search was intense. In these meetings, each member was given time to share his experiences during the week. Each one reported what he felt he had gained through the disciplines advocated by the organization.

We had specific books like textbooks that taught philosophies of Eastern culture and religion. I was fascinated by the altruistic principles that we studied and strived to achieve. It was my desire to reach up, to attain a higher level of life, and most of all, to find a way to make the unexplainable empty feeling inside of me go away.

I would dutifully carry out any disciplines requested by the leader of the week or given to us from our text. Some weeks, this meant fasting. Group members were asked to fast a meal or eat only certain foods. One time, I went on a three-day fast of eating only apples; this was supposed to be a cleansing fast. Another discipline was daily meditation. Every day without fail, I would go to my bedroom and sit on the floor with my legs crossed. I sat perfectly still and cleared my mind by pushing each thought away until I felt calm and peaceful. Peace would come, but I never could get away from the fact that the peace never lasted. I longed for a lasting peace, a refuge from the turmoil, loneliness, and pain of life.

I lived in a great place to practice this type of daily meditation. The job Mark held was caretaker of a park. Because of his job, we actually lived in the park. The morning hours of summer and the short, cold days of winter made the park a refuge, a hiding place. The quiet times were my favorite times. With one small child and a great big dog, I would walk through the park under the towering trees. I loved the crunching leaves under my feet and the sound of the wind blowing through the trees. One of the concrete picnic tables near a lake was the perfect place to sit and reflect.

Jennifer and I felt safe in the empty park. One of our security measures was our dog, Boo. He was half German shepherd and half husky. Boo was a beautiful dog and very intelligent. He was glad to be out of the fence and have free run of the park for a while. High poles held long-roped swings that occupied Jennifer while I sat at a picnic table under the trees. I would lift my face upward and look at the moss-draped trees forming arches against the sky. Sunlight filtered through the leaves and branches. It's like a cathedral, I thought.

Drinking in the beauty of the trees, the lake water, Boo running through the park, the moss hanging, and the wind blowing, I tried again to fill the emptiness inside. My spirit was trying to communicate with God, but I didn't know how to accomplish my desire. Prayer as I know it today was totally foreign to me then. I simply sat on the concrete table and feasted on the beauty and glory of God's creation, yearning for something I could not describe and did not understand.

For a while, the feast of nature appeased my appetite. Then the haunting questions would return: God, where are You? I'm looking for You. And where is Mark? Where is someone for me? Why must my life be so lonely even in marriage? This is my second marriage and life is no better. I just have a new set of problems.

We had lived in the park for a year and a half when Mark decided to change jobs. A new job meant we had to find a place to live. It would take time to coordinate new living quarters and a job as well. My friend Barbara and her husband were kind enough to let us stay with them for several weeks.

One night as we settled in to go to sleep, Mark whispered to me, "Mary, there's something I have to tell you."

"What is it?" I asked curiously.

"It's something I have needed to tell you for a long time, but I've been too afraid. I finally decided that I have to tell you because I can't bear the feelings of guilt anymore."

"Mark, what are you talking about? What is it?" I implored.

"You have to promise that you won't leave me, Mary. Please promise. I can't tell you until you promise me that."

"Mark, I can't promise something I know nothing about. What's going on?"

"I've been seeing many other women since we got married."

Time suspended for me. Mark was talking, but his words sounded hollow. I felt as if I were in an echo chamber. "What is he saying?" I whispered to myself. "I can't make out the words."

Momentarily, I surfaced from the chamber and heard Mark saying, " . . . more about it. It's very late, and I have to get up at four o'clock in the morning. Promise me that you will be here when I get off work so we can talk."

I lay in the darkness stunned and speechless. The moonlight caused the curtains to throw shadowed patterns on the ceiling and walls. I watched the changing patterns for a long time until sleep mercifully pushed the pain into tomorrow.

The sound of the alarm clock aroused my senses out of their numbed state. I pushed myself from the bed to join Barbara in the kitchen. We packed lunches for our husbands to take to work each day. The earliness of the hour relieved me from having to talk with Barbara. The kitchen light glared at us through the dark coolness of the early morning. We scrambled eggs and let them cook with bacon while we made sandwiches with Barbara's homemade bread.

Mark and Steve came to the table dressed for work and ready for breakfast. The four of us sat around the table, and again I was thankful for the surrounding darkness and brevity of time. Barbara's husband and Mark exchanged sentences between bites of food. Barbara made occasional comments, and I was hoping no one noticed my inability to join in with the small talk. My thoughts seemed to be in slow motion, and I had to work to keep a normal look on my face. There was neither time nor place for a private conversation with Mark. I would have to wait until late in the afternoon.

When it was time for the men to go, I followed Mark to the door. Mark turned to me and whispered, "Please be here when I get back. I want to talk to you."

"I'll be here," I answered, having no idea of what else to say or where I could go.

With the men gone for the day, Barbara and I turned to go clean up the kitchen. I wasn't ready to share my emotional pain, so I mentioned Barbara's bread recipe. Barbara loved healthful food and was always ready to talk about her stone-ground wheat bread or her organic vegetable garden. Barbara was now on her favorite subject, and I didn't have to try to talk.

Instead of going back to bed in the early morning, Barbara and I would exercise in the living room after cleaning up the kitchen. We would nap later with the children rather than lose this little bit of time while they were still sleeping. Jennifer was now five years old, and Barbara had two children smaller than Jennifer.

The morning light was beginning to dawn while we were exercising. I strained to pay attention to Barbara's conversation. I did not want to tell her of Mark's confession the previous night; my thoughts were too disoriented. There were too many things to sort through, and I wanted to sort through them by myself before I talked with anyone else.

"Mary, what's wrong with you?" Barbara asked as she came to an abrupt standstill from jumping and twisting.

My face broke; the tears flowed. There was nothing I could do to stop them. I sat down in a dining room chair and laid my head on the table.

"Mary, what's the matter?"

Sobs choked down any attempted answers, and Barbara sat helplessly beside me trying to understand the garbled words. She left for a minute and came back with a box of tissue. "Now, Mary, what are you trying to say about Mark? What has he done?"

I ran out of tears and lay still for a moment. Then I sat up straight and told Barbara in a monotone voice, "He's been seeing other women ever since we got married. For two years he's been unfaithful to me, and I knew nothing about it until last night."

"Last night," Barbara gasped. "You mean he told you something like that last night? He waited until you didn't have a place of your own and then gives you that kind of information? I can't believe it. Mary, what are you going to do?"

"I don't know. I haven't had time to think about it yet or figure things out. I have no idea what to do."

"You can't stay with him, Mary. Surely you are not thinking of that. I wouldn't do it, no sir. Two years of unfaithfulness is not a one-time fling."

"Barbara, I don't know what to think. I can't think straight right now. I don't have any place to go. Anyway, Mark wants to talk to me when he gets back today."

"Look, Mary, you don't owe Mark anything right now. If it was me, I wouldn't be here when he got back."

Jennifer came around the corner rubbing her eyes. "Hi, Mommy," she mumbled.

I put Jennifer on my lap and glanced at Barbara to say, "We'll talk later."

Soon Barbara's children were up too. We went through round two with breakfast and kitchen work. The morning wore on slowly until we had the children ready to play for a little while.

The morning routine had given me some time to think. Barbara's words kept returning to my mind. She's right,

I thought. I shouldn't be here when he gets back. He chose to give me that news when there was no time to talk. "Barbara," I said out loud, "where can I go?"

"I've been thinking, Mary. Mark went with my husband in our truck. We can put your things in your car, and you can go stay with your sister until you figure out what to do on your own."

Phyllis shared a house with another girl. I called Phyllis, giving her a brief account of my situation, and she readily offered her home to me and Jennifer.

Staying with Phyllis enabled me to have time to get a job and find my own apartment. Having used survival tactics before, it didn't take long for me to become independent again. Mark came to see me periodically and tried to patch things up. My wounds were too gaping to be patched by any person. I needed God, but instead of searching for Him, I was still just wanting answers. I had not yet discovered that searching for God and searching for answers were not the same thing. Answers by themselves can be wrong.

Chapter Four

Strike Three?

It had been months since I had gone to a group meeting. The meeting place had changed to Jerry and Corrine's house. On Tuesday evening I knocked on their door. Everyone welcomed me back and asked where I had been for so long. I gave a minimal explanation of my divorce from Mark. It felt good to be back among friends again.

We went on with our meeting. After all, the basis of these gatherings was to study and discuss philosophies and concepts that we thought held the answers to life's dilemmas. I didn't know it yet, but one group member was especially interested in my dilemma.

Friday evening my phone rang. "This is Bob."

"Bob?" I repeated after him.

"From the study group," he explained.

"Oh, Bob! Well, hello."

"I'd like to take you to the ball game Friday night. Would you like to go?"

I had never looked at Bob as a date before. The idea needed time to gel. "I'm busy this week, Bob. Maybe some other time," I replied.

The next week Bob called several times and I finally relented; we had a date. I knew Bob well since we had been in the same group for almost two years. Bob had two boys from a previous marriage. His oldest boy, Dwayne, was seven. Keven, at five years old, was the same age as Jennifer.

Our date consisted of taking the children to the park for a game of hide and seek among the trees. I stood behind a thick trunk and peeked around the side. No one was in sight. The anticipation of waiting for someone to make a move was fun. I stood very still and giggled quietly. I was twenty-five years old and had already been through financial strain, loneliness, illness, and two divorces. I relished a moment of laughter and fun.

Peeking around the tree again, I saw Dwayne dash across the clearing. Bob darted out from behind another tree and chased after him. Keven and Jennifer were too young to adhere strictly to the game plan. They came out from behind their respective trees and joined in the fun of running. Bob looked around for me. I must have made a move because I saw the recognition of my hiding place in his face. He had spotted me.

I took off running in the other direction. Bob, who is almost eight years my senior, was thirty-three. He didn't look the type to move fast. Glancing over my shoulder, I could see him gaining ground quickly. The three children were running behind at staggered paces. I ran as fast as I could, enjoying every minute of it. Two big hands caught me at the waist and pulled me down.

We tumbled to the ground, and the children piled on top of us.

We got up from the ground laughing and panting for air. "Let's go feed the ducks," Bob suggested.

"That's a good idea," I quickly agreed. "We can catch our breath."

Bob and I sauntered across the grass over to the pond. Dwayne, Keven, and Jennifer, who had energy to burn, were running crisscross in front of us and all around. A wooden bench with black iron armrests was nestled among an inset of flower beds filled with blossoms. We sat on the bench and watched the three youngsters throw the bread crumbs that Bob had brought in a bag.

Jennifer still frightened easily. When a duck came too close, she would squeal and run away from the pond. Dwayne and Keven were normal boys and took delight in the opportunity of having a little girl around to tease. They called her a scaredy cat and threw the bread crumbs near the banks of the pond, making the ducks come closer.

On the way home from the park, we stopped for an ice cream cone. Jennifer's milk allergy prevented her from eating ice cream, so she enjoyed a small Coke and some French fries. I looked at the three children on this date and thought how nice it was that Bob's planning had included them. Bob had been a single man for three years, and when the boys were with him, they went where he went. I appreciated his care for his children. I knew from my own daughter that children from broken homes need as much attention, love, and stability as they can receive.

The five of us dated for a few months, and then Bob asked me to marry him. I asked him for time to think. That was preposterous because I could not think straight at the time anyway. In fact, I had not been thinking straight for years. I had no compass for direction in my life.

As I tried to ferret out some sense in my muddled mind during the next couple of days, Bob went out of town on a business trip. Bob was (and still is) a calm, even-tempered man, and his absence unnerved me. When circumstances called for independence and responsibility, I had always risen to the occasion, but this time I felt an unraveling. The picture of life I had mentally painted at sweet sixteen was nowhere around. When Bob came back to town I said, "Yes."

We were married in a church that we had been visiting. The church was large and located in the metropolitan area. It was known for its teachings on reincarnation, mind control, and becoming at one with God, which agreed with what Bob and I had been studying and practicing through the group meetings.

The wedding was small, with only our children and two couples in attendance. My friends Barbara and Steve and Bob's friends Connye and Steve came to stand with us. We walked through the main church building to get to the chapel. The minister was waiting for us as we took our places at the front. Dwayne, Keven, and Jennifer sat quietly in a pew behind us and watched wide-eyed. The ceremony was short with no fanfare. I, for one, wasn't looking for a great wedding; I wanted a lasting marriage. Bob took my face in his hands, leaned down, and kissed me. We turned to gather our three children together. We were a family.

Bob had recently moved into a new house. I did not have to contend with feeling that the house belonged to his previous family. We came through the front door into a large, empty living room furnished only with one bean-bag chair on the dark blue carpet. Bob explained that he wanted new furniture in his new house, which was fine with me. We needed all the freshness we could muster to start building a life together.

A gray brick fireplace on the far wall gave warmth to the empty room. The kids didn't mind the emptiness. It gave them space to tumble and roll.

The squared kitchen, complete with breakfast nook and bay window, was a delight after those crunched apartment kitchens. ". . . and this is your stove and here's your dishwasher," Bob was saying as if he were a tour guide.

A long hallway aligned the bedrooms in the L-shaped house. Dwayne and Keven had separate rooms until now. One of our first purchases was a set of bunk beds. The boys had to team up in a bedroom so that Jennifer could have a room.

The master bedroom was so big that I think one of the apartments I had lived in could have fit in there. The queen-size bed was accompanied by a makeshift table supporting an old black lamp. I was undaunted by the sparse furnishings; the space of the house made me feel that I had moved into sheer luxury.

A flowered courtyard offset the outside length of the hallway. Lilac-colored crepe myrtle blossoms brushed against the window of the master bedroom. We put an old rocking chair by that window. In time that spot became a favorite of mine.

For the first time since Jennifer was born, I was able to be a stay-at-home mother. Jennifer was so used to being rushed early in the mornings that I never could get her to slow down when she was eating breakfast and getting ready for kindergarten. It was also a new experience for her to come home at noon instead of going to day care.

Another new experience for both Jennifer and me was Christmas. Bob and I were married in early December, and Christmas was upon us with three children to shop for. This was one date we were going on by ourselves. Bob took me to a toy store. I never knew such a thing existed; my frugal life could not accommodate a toy store. We walked into the huge storehouse, and I entered another world. I gazed at row upon row of toys, books, puzzles, and games. The store was brightly decorated, and the Christmas trimmings accentuated the glittering lights and whimsical walls. It was a fantasy world.

Bob made a study of remote-control cars and baseball gloves, while I visually took in the surroundings. He made a few selections as we meandered up and down the aisles. We turned a corner, and shelves of dolls with accompanying paraphernalia stretched before us. I looked up at Bob as wide eyed as a child. "Go ahead," he said. "What would you like for Jennifer?"

"Wow!" I exclaimed like a six-year-old. Memories of the torn paper pieces and catalog pictures I had cut out for dolls twenty years earlier fluttered through my mind. Then I remembered the Barbie doll on my eleventh birthday and the scraps of fabric I used to drape around it.

I picked out a family of dolls for Jennifer and put them in the basket. I was through shopping. To my amazement Bob began putting the doll accessories in the basket; in went the little clothes, the tiny furniture, and last but not least, a big box that contained a doll house to be assembled. My eyes widened further as I looked at the bulging basket. This would be a Christmas to remember.

Christmas Eve was a late night. The living room became a toy factory. Bob put batteries in Dwayne and Keven's cars and began work on the doll house while I watched with excitement. I could hardly wait for him to finish so I could play with it. Finally, he stood with satisfaction and stretched his knees. I sat in front of the doll house and arranged the petite chairs and tables. Then I dressed each doll and placed it in the facsimile of a living room.

"Dad, Mom, get up. It's time for Christmas," came the morning call of three perky people.

We put on warm robes and headed for the living room. Dwayne, Keven, and Jennifer scurried to the tree and dug in. "Wait a minute," said Bob. "Let's open things one at a time. That's how my family always did on Christmas morning."

"But, Bob, my family always just jumped in. It's chaotic fun. Can we do that?" I asked tentatively.

"Well, I guess we can this year," he responded kindly.

"Oh, good! Come on kids, let's go," I encouraged them. This was a novel Christmas, and I wanted to wring every bit of enjoyment out of it that I could. It wasn't just the presents that made that Christmas unique; it was the new family feeling of having a dad, a mom, and three children all together.

We discovered that Jennifer was not one to play with dolls. She surveyed the doll house briefly and changed the doll clothes a time or two. That was the extent of doll appeal for her. I, however, spent some time with those dolls until my memories were sated and the dolls became only decorations for the corner of Jennifer's bedroom. It was a good Christmas.

The following days were busy with cooking, laundry, and kids. Kindergarten scheduling broke up the days, plus Dwayne and Keven were often there. The boys lived about three miles away with their mother. Their townhouse was en route to Bob's job. In many instances a divorced dad sees his children only two weekends per month, but Bob picked up his boys every weekend and additional evenings during the week.

It was okay with me that Dwayne and Keven were at our house so often. Having my own child from a previous marriage, I was sympathetic to Bob's desire to be with his children. Complications did arise, however, from the stress of two families welded together. A welded seam is not as smooth as a seamless unit.

A favorite pastime of Dwayne and Keven was sorting baseball cards. The kitchen floor was the best place to do this because of the smooth tile; at least, that is what they claimed. These cards were everywhere, and Keven even learned to read by sorting baseball cards with his older brother. I tiptoed through the stacks on the floor to fix meals.

It was almost February when my patience began to wear thin. The strength and stamina of my teenage days was gone due to the stress of the more recent years. I tired very easily and stepped on one baseball card too many. I started to cry and went to the bedroom to lie down. When I closed my eyes all I could see was baseball cards. The kitchen floor had been perfect for the boys' hobby while their dad was single, but now it was time to relocate the card-cataloging project.

The tiredness I was feeling deepened, and I went to the doctor. The lab test came back positive. Bob and I were expecting a baby of our own. This was great news to me, because I wanted family ties. I felt that this baby would unite our patchwork family with a common bond.

The next seven months flew by. Dwayne and Keven were on different Little League teams because of their ages. Practice nights did not coincide; hence we were on the ball field an average of six nights a week. Bob was an assistant coach on both teams.

Bob and I were still in the weekly study group where we had met. On Tuesday evenings after ball practice, we managed to have time to join our friends for discussion and study. The meetings had moved to our house, which now had some furniture in the living room. By meeting in our own home I was able to put the boys and Jennifer to bed and get to bed earlier myself for a little extra rest.

The tenets of this study group had become the foundation of my life. I subsisted on the principle of working out problems so that I would not have to go through them again in another life. I strove to attain a high level of consciousness with the expectation of becoming a person full of patience, love, strength, and endurance. I had read that the attainment of that perfect state would bring total peace and fulfillment. That was my goal.

Bob was on the same track. With his even-tempered qualities and management capabilities, he had become the chairman for our local area. The spiritual belief we adhered to was the common denominator in our lives. It had been our meeting ground and had become our daily practice together.

Again, I could not explain the empty feeling I had inside. One day I picked up an armful of shirts to iron and took stock of my current life while I pressed them. The formal dining room was a great place to iron. Separating the living room from the kitchen, it was in a well-lit area in the front of the house. There was a piano against a wall that was intended for a china hutch, but three children and one pending took financial priority over dining-room furniture.

The minimal concentration required for ironing allowed me time to think. Bob was a good man. He had a job that kept him busy, and he gave a lot of attention to his two boys. There was a place in my heart that I wanted Bob to fill up, but it was a place that no human can fill. Where is that peace? I wondered.

Bob arrived home from work and interrupted my reverie. "There's a storm coming, Mary. A hurricane is out in the gulf. I'm not taking any chances; you're going to the hospital," he stated in a tone that left no room for dispute.

The two entrances to our subdivision flooded easily and drained slowly. The potential of being blocked in for days at a time was evident. I gave Bob no argument. The doctor had moved the baby's due date up two weeks, and I had been having contractions that day. My bag was packed, and Bob drove me to the hospital.

Jeffery made a safe entrance into the world at 3:42 A.M. The storm had passed, and the nurse brought me a small, tightly wrapped bundle. Jeffery's eyes were squeezed shut as if he had determined that he was going to get some sleep. I held him up and gave him ever-so-gentle shakes, trying to get him to open his eyes. I laughed at the little puckered face that adamantly continued to sleep.

"You can go home," announced the doctor the next day.

"Oh, no! Please don't send me home yet," I pleaded. "When I get home, my husband will go back to work and there are three young children to take care of, plus the baby. My mom and sisters work, and I won't have enough help. Please let me stay a couple of days."

Did the doctor think I was strange? I wondered if he got such requests very often. The wisdom of that request was revealed when I had postpartum contractions for four days and arrived home still in a state of exhaustion. Bob carried the baby into the house and returned to the car to help me. Leaning heavily on his arms, I made it to the bedroom. I had enough awareness to notice that Bob had cleaned the house immaculately. He put me to bed with Jeff tucked in beside me. I don't remember the next few days.

I took up the basic household tasks as soon as I gained enough strength to function. It was a joy to take care of our new family member. I had missed a lot of Jennifer's babyhood by having to work, so I relished each moment with this baby. Jeffery was born in September when Jennifer was beginning first grade. Another six years of rocking, diapers, nursery rhymes, and games of Fish and Candyland was beginning. I sat in the chair by my favorite window cuddling Jeffery every day. We rocked and rocked while I sang made-up songs to him. Fall was turning into winter again, and the crepe myrtle bush was bare, but it was still my favorite window.

The day came when we had to trade bedrooms with Dwayne and Keven. Since the new baby was a boy, the master bedroom was the only way to accommodate the young males in our family. We could not yet afford bedroom furniture, so we easily fit into the smaller room.

We moved the queen-size bed, the makeshift table, and the shoe boxes that served as dresser drawers. I glanced at my favorite window and thought of the years ahead before that spot would be mine again.

The rocker moved to the living room, where Jeffery and I continued our daily routine. Between spontaneous lyric productions I resumed my inner dialogue that had been temporarily disrupted with Jeffery's birth. Even with my new baby to hold, the haunting questions would surface in my mind. Where was that elusive peace? I was still an ardent reader of books. The books were always in the realm of spiritual and philosophical thought. Why couldn't I find whatever I was looking for? Then I thought, What exactly *am* I looking for?

That question brought focus to my searching. It dawned on me that I had been looking for peace, health, happiness, and love. For the first time since that innovative prayer in my red-carpeted apartment so long ago, I realized that I had not been talking to God. God and spiritual thoughts were an integral part of my life, but I had been talking about God and reading men's ideas of God. I had been looking everywhere except up.

I got on my knees and prayed for the second time in my own words. "God, I've tried to find You and I can't. Would You please come and find me? Amen." I knelt there and cried, having no words or understanding of God. Bob was in the other room with his boys. I felt alone. He was a good husband, but I needed something more.

Chapter Five

Mardel

The bedroom was completely empty. The bed, makeshift table, and shoe boxes were gone. I was standing by the closet door with a shawl that belonged to my mother draped over my shoulders. The bedroom door was ajar, and I could hear the study group meeting in the living room.

Movement from the other direction caught my eye, and I turned toward the window. It was very dark outside. The moonlight was dim, and I could see the stars glimmering in the sky. A majestic white horse was running in circles outside my window. I stood transfixed gazing at him. I could see the powerful muscles working in his body. His white mane flowed with the force of his stride. Around and around he went. The power in the scene was mesmerizing.

I turned momentarily toward the bedroom door. In an instant I made a decision before I even realized there was a choice. I took a quick step forward and closed the door, completely shutting out the meeting that was taking place in the living room. Immediately I heard a resounding crash of breaking glass. I whirled around to see the beautiful horse leaping with full force through the window. The shattering glass sprayed through the air. The front legs and breast of the horse were above me, and in a millisecond of time, I knew I was going to be killed. Then everything went black.

I waited as the seconds passed. I knew that the horse had landed on me and that I was dead. Time was suspended, and I could only wait to see what would happen next. The dark stillness lingered, and then my eyes opened.

I was lying in the bed with Bob beside me. The hair on my neck and arms was straight on end, and I had broken out in a slight sweat.

I had never had a dream like that before and have never had one since. Every facet of the dream was three-dimensional and unforgettable. I did not care what time of the night it was; I was going to wake up Bob.

"Wha, what? What's going on? What's the matter?" Bob slurred as I shook him from a deep sleep.

"Bob, listen! I just had a dream. You've got to hear it, right now. It can't wait," I insisted.

"C'mon, Mary, it's four in the morning. You can tell me tomorrow," he said, attempting to turn over.

"No, you don't understand. This can't wait. Bob, I died. You know people don't die in their dreams. You always wake up before the bogyman gets you, right? Well, I died. How can that be? What does it mean? Listen, there was this incredible horse, and he came through the window and killed me. He was all white and beautiful and powerful. The dream was so real that I could see and feel and hear everything. I heard the window break and felt the wind of the horse leaping in the air. What does it mean?''

Bob was fully awake by this time. He listened as I detailed the dream again and again until I could settle down. Bob had no understanding of the dream either, but he suggested some people for me to contact later that might have some insight into the dream's purpose and meaning.

It didn't take too long for Bob to go back to sleep, since he had only heard a verbal rendition of my dream. The impact of the three-dimensional dream left me awake most of the remaining night.

When morning light came I busied myself with chores so I wouldn't rudely awaken friends before the breakfast hour. When nine o'clock finally arrived, I picked up the phone and began calling selected study-group members. I recounted the vivid details and sequence of events in the dream without hesitation. Each listener had his or her own interpretation of the scenes and symbols described. Differing opinions left my questions unanswered, but I could not shake off the unsettling effects or the clarity of the vision.

Two days after the dream I took Jennifer to her Thursday afternoon ballet class. The thirty-minute class did not allow enough time to go home or run errands, so I stayed in the front room of the building with other mothers. Looking for a place to sit and hold Jeffery during the wait, I noticed a thin young woman with sandy-colored hair who was sitting quietly by herself. In some instances I can be very shy, but when I see someone who looks lonesome or uncomfortable my desire to help overrides my shyness.

"Hi, I'm Mary. I haven't seen you here before. Is this your daughter's first class?" I ventured.

"No, she is making up the class that she missed Tuesday. My name is Diane. Your baby is so cute," she commented as she held up a finger for Jeffery to grasp.

A baby's presence quickly melts the ice when meeting new people. The conversation flowed more smoothly with Jeffery's innocent aid. "Do you have other children?" I asked. The question was ordinary enough to facilitate a casual meeting.

"No, it's just myself and my little girl," Diane replied. A note of despondency hung in her voice. Her eyes glanced off to the side. It looked as if the slightest tap would crack the fragile expression on her face.

Being one who understood concealed pain, I felt that I had the right to offer her a moment of friendship if she decided to take it. "All alone, Diane? Are you divorced?"

"No. My husband worked for an oil company. There was a major explosion last year, and he was killed," Diane answered with trained emotions.

My heart skipped a beat, and I felt a jab of inner pain at the thought of Diane's sorrow. Instantly, I wanted to comfort her. The philosophies that I had clung to for life support were well versed in my mind and surfaced with speed. The next twenty minutes passed quickly, and our daughters came running to rejoin us.

Diane was interested in the conversation. In despair she was searching for comfort and answers. "I want to hear more, Mary. Will you visit me?"

"Sure, just name the time and day. I'll be there. Do you live nearby?"

"I want to talk to you soon, Mary. Listen, I'm going

to the farmer's market tomorrow with a lady I met earlier this week. She's been talking with me too. Will you go with us?"

"I don't know that lady, Diane. She didn't invite me. I would feel like an intruder."

"No, it's okay. She's a friendly lady, and I know she wouldn't mind. I'll call her and ask if it's okay, then I'll call you tonight. Would that make you feel better about it?"

"Definitely," I answered. "I will wait to hear from you, and if this doesn't work out, we'll get together on another day."

I drove home reflecting on the conversation with Diane and the disaster of instant widowhood. At the thought of spending a day with the other lady whom Diane had met, the shy streak in me began to surface and brought that butterfly feeling to my stomach.

Friday morning Jennifer left for school, and I set about to make beds and dress Jeffery for an outing. Diane had called the night before and confirmed the arrangements for our day at the market. At the sound of a horn honking, I peeked out the window to see a big Buick in my driveway. I scooped up the diaper bag and Jeffery in his infant carrier, locked the door, and headed for the car.

Diane met me on the sidewalk and brought me to her acquaintance, who was in the driver's seat. "This is Mardel," she said with a slight wave of her hand toward the car's occupant.

Mardel looked to be in her fifties. She was a tall, trim woman with very long gray hair that was neatly wrapped into a French twist. "Pleased to meet you," she said with a smile. "Get in and let's go. It's a long way to the other side of Houston."

There was no question as to who was in command of this trip. The older woman was a no-nonsense person whose statements were concise and directive. Diane resumed her position in the passenger's side of the front seat, and I went into the back seat where I could strap Jeffery's carrier beside me.

Mardel began a line of small talk, compensating with ease for her two quiet-natured passengers. No wonder Diane wanted me to go on this trip with her, I thought to myself. She probably was unable to say no to this woman and wanted a companion to cling to. This was easy for me to understand because I would do the same thing.

Although Mardel was an authoritative woman, she was not unkind. As we neared our destination, Diane and I began to relax. The conversation was interesting as Mardel informed us of the advantages and wisdom of eating what she called "God's food," referring to natural-grown foods without a lot of processing. Mardel did seem vibrant and energetic. My friend Barbara came to my mind. She was like that too. Barbara could run rings around me.

Maybe there's something to this, I pondered. My declining health gave me reason to listen more carefully. Although I was functioning and performing basic tasks every day, I constantly battled extreme fatigue and an all-over aching feeling. Most of my afternoons were spent in bed to store up enough strength to cook dinner and make it through the evening hours.

We arrived at the market, and Mardel escorted us through her familiar shopping route. Diane and I looked on as Mardel perused the many tables loaded with fruits and vegetables and made her selections according to freshness and ripeness. As she shopped, Mardel would wave or stop and chat with the vendors. It was obvious that this place was a regular routine in her life.

The market was large, and we spent the entire morning investigating the scope and contents of it. When Mardel had given us a complete tour and had bought what she needed, it was time for lunch. As we got back in the car Mardel extended an invitation to lunch at her house. Her description of homemade bread and freshly prepared food was inviting indeed, and both Diane and I took her up on it.

The ride back across town brought a turn in our subject matter. The morning had served its purpose in our becoming acquainted with each other. Mardel opened up the conversation to more pressing needs, specifically the realm of how to cope with life's tragedies as in Diane's current situation.

Immediately my thoughts picked up speed. The conversation was veering toward the topics that made me come alive. Mardel began to talk about the Bible. She also shared the experience of losing a son in death and offered words of comfort to Diane.

Discussions on spiritual matters always dissolved my shy streak. I joined heartily in the conversation, making contributions anytime Mardel would pause. The things Mardel said sparked the most-used portion of my memory banks. Between the two of us the verbiage flowed unhaltingly, and Diane hungrily devoured the contents.

We turned into the driveway of a nice brick home on a tree-lined street. Mardel brought us into the house through the garage. It was easier to unload her purchases near the kitchen area of the house. I got Jeffery situated and went to help Mardel and Diane carry in bags and boxes. Weakling or not, I wasn't about to sit back and watch other people work. There was a commanding little voice in me that said, "Do your part."

When everything was carried in, Mardel offered bar stools to me and Diane. We perched on the stools and leaned on the counter that divided the living room from the kitchen. A long strip of stained-glass carvings, the product of one of Mardel's hobbies, hung from the ceiling above the counter, adding character to the rooms. A pot of herb tea flavored with lemon and honey was steeping on the stove while Mardel assembled bountiful sandwiches complete with bright red tomato slices and crisp green lettuce.

Mardel and I continued our verbal volley through our delicious lunch. As the three of us set about to clean up, the conversation was in my court. I began a discourse on the cycles of life and how to be an overcomer of the current pain so that one does not have to repeat the circumstances in another life.

Mardel froze where she was standing. For more than a hour we had been agreeably sharing information. With unexpected abruptness the entire atmosphere changed. Mardel stood erect and firm. Her gray-blue eyes bore into me. "No," she stated flatly. "You are wrong, Mary."

I stood across from her. My mind went blank and then began to reel. Wrong? What does she mean, wrong? I've been spouting this stuff for years, and nobody has ever said it was wrong. Some people weren't interested in my dissertations, and others asked for further explanations, but no one ever said it was wrong.

"I have some information you can look at," Mardel

was saying when I tuned back in to her words. "This philosophy that you have is not of God, Mary. Start reading the New Testament. Begin in the Gospel of John and read straight through Revelation. Go look for yourself."

Mardel's words had a power behind them that was incomprehensible to me. Explosions were taking place inside of me that I could not account for. There seemed to be no reason for her simple, short statements to cause that much destruction to my foundation.

A knock at Mardel's door interrupted her further explanations, and she opened the door to two of her friends. After brief introductions, Mardel commented on the conversation that had been taking place. With only a few sentences from Mardel, her friends were nodding that they understood. How can they understand so quickly? I'm still in the dark and I was here before these two, I thought in my puzzled mind.

One of Mardel's friends suggested that we pray together. The two ladies and Mardel grasped hands in a semicircle. The obvious space remaining let Diane and me know that we were supposed to follow suit. Diane had been sitting on the bar stool. She climbed down and joined the others. I took the last spot, making the circle complete.

A lady named Carolyn began a prayer. Everyone else was quiet, and I was listening intently. The next lady picked up where Carolyn left off, and she said a short verbal prayer. I realized that each one would be expected to pray. Panic seized me. These people were making up prayers, and I had only done that twice in my life, both times being in private. Around the circle went the prayer.

I'm not sure how well Diane did at praying out loud because I was getting too worried as my turn came near.

A momentary silence told me it was my turn. I was already radically shaken by the previous conversation with Mardel. There was no time to think or figure out how to pray the way those ladies did. I had no idea what I was going to do. "Our Father which art in heaven, hallowed be Thy name . . . ," I heard myself saying; it was all that I knew to do. I continued the rote prayer that I knew so well, but this time it was very different. Never in my life had I said it with such meaning from my heart. Praying had never made me cry before, but this time tears rolled freely down my cheeks.

When we dropped each other's hands, I quickly wiped my face. I did not understand what was going on or what was happening to me. I wanted to get out of there. I wanted to go home. Diane's car was at Mardel's house, and she had mentioned earlier that she would take me home. "Diane, our daughters will be coming home from school. We had better be on our way, okay?"

Diane and I said our goodbyes to Mardel and her friends. I gathered up Jeffery and we left. Looking anxiously at Diane, I surmised that she was not conscious of the extent of my turmoil. That's good, I thought. I didn't want to look like a total fool to my new friend. Diane did most of the talking on this short trip.

"Thanks for the ride, Diane," I said as she dropped me off at my house. She didn't stay since her daughter would be home from school soon.

I went in the front door and ran right into Bob, who was walking by on his way to the kitchen. "You're home early today! Oh, I'm so glad to see you!" I exclaimed though my arms were too full to give him a hug.

"What happened to you?" he asked before greeting me. "Your face is as white as a sheet."

"I met a lady today. She said the things that I believe about God and life after death are wrong."

"Why should that bother you? Everybody's entitled to their own belief," he answered with pure logic.

"I don't know why. I can't figure it out, but my insides feel like a hurricane has hit with crashing waves. Here's Jeff. I have to go lie down for a while," I said as I handed Jeffery over to Bob.

The bedroom provided a retreat from people and activity. I closed the door and lowered my trembling body onto the bed. I tried to quit shaking by lying still and taking slow, deep breaths. The magnitude of Mardel's words surfaced as my thoughts began their parade: How can I be wrong? If that's true, then everything that has held me together through pain and trouble has been a false hope. If that is taken away, what is there to replace it? What's right? What's truth? Oh, God, where's peace? What if Mardel is right? That's it! That's the problem—Mardel set up an absolute. She didn't say she merely disagreed with me. She said I was wrong. That means one of us must concede.

My thoughts tumbled and rolled. A crack in the foundation of my belief system was not a minor incident. The beliefs that I adhered to had been sufficient enough to dampen fleeting suicidal notions through the years. I felt as if a rug had been ripped out from under my feet. What would hold me up?

It was soon time to get up and go cook supper. My shoulder-length hair was disheveled. I lifted my hair on each side and anchored it with combs in one of my incessant attempts to contain it. Thinking that I had squelched the thought parade, I was surprised when one more impression darted through my mind as I opened the bedroom door: "Read the New Testament; just read it."

Chapter Six

The Living Word

"Good night," Bob and I called out the door as the last group member left our house. We turned back to the living room to pick up the cups and plates left from the post-meeting snack. Then Bob went to take a shower while I picked up our books to reshelve them. Since selected passages of Scripture were part of our study series, Bob had purchased a Bible for us. I slipped the Bible into its place between some other books. Instead of turning away to go get ready for bed, I stood there looking at the cover spine of the Book I had never read, the Bible.

She told me to read it, I thought for a moment as I remembered Mardel's distant words. Eight months had passed since I had seen her or spoken with her. The absolute that Mardel had set up by stating that I held wrong beliefs about God angered me. Mardel was wise in leaving me alone to thresh out my thoughts and feelings.

Tonight, the anger is gone, I realized with a new

tenderness of heart as the vestiges of anger melted away. I see now that I've really been afraid during all these months. It's like Mardel pulled a thread that began to unravel everything that I have believed. The answers that I had collected to life's troubles are blank spaces again. I'm back at square one. Read the Gospel of John, she said.

I pulled the Bible back off the shelf and carried it with me to the bedroom. Okay, I will start tonight . . . two chapters per night, I decided. I will see who's right.

After getting myself ready for bed, I turned on the bedside lamp and put the Bible in front of my pillow. I lay on my stomach and thumbed through the pages to find the Gospel of John. Once I located it, I propped my chin in my hands and began reading. I read slowly and with wonder. It didn't make a lot of sense to me, but for some reason I felt good that I had finally made the decision to read it. After two chapters I closed the Bible and turned out the light. That's all for tonight, I thought to myself. I want to take my time and try to understand what I'm reading.

Two chapters per night became a routine. Week after week, I read the Bible every night without fail. Nothing astounding seemed to be happening, but I occasionally read a verse that reinforced what I had believed for many years or a verse that reinforced Mardel's beliefs. I developed a system of initialing the margins with either my initials or Mardel's initials depending on my findings.

In the Book of Romans, I put Mardel's initials beside the twenty-third verse of chapter three. It stated, "For all have sinned, and come short of the glory of God." I felt compelled to pause and look closely at that verse. It was definitely not reinforcing the idea that everyone is working to become at one with God; in fact, it stated the opposite. I looked at the verse again and focused on the word "sinned." My world had lost the clarity of black and white and had become gray. Actions were not viewed as right or wrong but were chosen according to circumstances. The word "sinned" reintroduced the possibility of literally wrong actions back into my thoughts. I underlined the word and continued reading.

One day after this regimen of Bible reading began, I heard a large truck pull to a stop almost in front of my house. Looking out the window I could see the orange cab of a moving van. "Ah, new neighbors. I wonder what they're like. I wonder if they have any kids. Are they old or young? I hope they're nice," I muttered to myself almost in one breath.

Later in the day my doorbell rang. I opened the door to a tall, attractive woman in her early thirties. Her short brown hair was neatly arranged, and large framed glasses highlighted her noticeably pretty eyes. "Hello," she said in a clear but very soft tone. "I'm Sandy, your new neighbor. It will be a day or two before I get a phone put in; may I use yours?"

"Of course! Come right in. My name is Mary, and I'm very glad to meet you. There's a phone in the kitchen. Make yourself at home," I answered with a wave of the hand toward the kitchen.

When Sandy finished her phone call, we exchanged information. "I have three boys," she said in her quiet, breathy voice. "Two are teenagers, and my youngest is eight years old."

"My husband, Bob, has two boys, ages ten and eight. I have an eight-year-old daughter, and this one's our baby," I responded while scooping up Jeffery as he toddled between us.

Jeffery flashed a million-dollar smile that would be hard for anyone to resist. Sandy and I delighted him by grinning back.

"We are moving here from a neighboring Houston suburb," Sandy explained. "This is the dream house that we have been saving up a long time to buy, and we're excited to be moving into it."

"That's great!" I responded enthusiastically. "This is a nice neighborhood. You'll like it. The only thing is, most of the ladies around here work, and it's like a ghost town in the daytime."

"Oh, I know people here who go to the same church where my family goes. They live around the corner. I've known them for years and they are good friends of mine. The lady's name is Priscilla."

"What an advantage you have to move in with ready-made friends," I answered.

Before Sandy left I said, "Come back anytime. I'm here during the day, and you are welcome to use the phone or come for anything that you need."

Sandy went back to her moving project, and I didn't see her again until the next day, when she came to borrow the phone again. We had another brief talk.

"I appreciate your hospitality, Mary. I want to invite you to my house next week when I have everything settled from the move. Priscilla will be there along with some other ladies we know from our church. We meet once a week for Bible study. Will you come?" Sandy asked.

"Yes! I just started reading the Bible a couple of months ago, and I don't understand it. Do you understand it? Can you help me?" I asked with eagerness.

Sandy smiled at me and said, "I've been reading the Bible for many years, Mary. I'm sure my friends and I can help you, but more important than that, the Lord will help you."

The Lord, I thought to myself. That's what Mardel called God. I remember that now.

"You come next Thursday at ten o'clock in the morning," Sandy said. "We'll be looking for you,"

"Can I bring Jeff? I don't have any place else to take him," I explained.

"Bring him with you. We have someone to watch the small children," Sandy answered as she turned to leave.

"Thanks. I'll be there," I called to her.

The following Thursday morning I waited until right at ten o'clock before going to Sandy's house. I didn't want to be the first one to arrive for the Bible study, and all I had to do was walk next door.

When Sandy's door opened, a woman with silver-toned frosted hair and a shiny clean face with naturally pink cheeks greeted me. "Hi!" she blurted with friendly fervor. "I'm Sandy's friend, Priscilla. You must be Mary. Come on in. We're ready to start."

Stepping into the foyer, I was at eye level with Priscilla, whose pleasingly plump form accentuated her beautiful smile and affability. Priscilla led me past the formal dining room on the right and into the family room. Sandy and her group of five friends gave me a warm welcome. One of the ladies ushered Jeffery into the bedroom designated for child care.

I took a seat on one of the two couches flanking the fireplace and looked up at the high, vaulted ceiling. The room was inviting and cozy with rich chocolate-colored carpet and earth-tone furnishings. Pretty plates of sliced fruit and snack cakes lined the bar between the kitchen and family room. At the end of the bar, an urn bubbled and churned, filling the air with the aroma of fresh coffee.

"Help yourselves to some refreshments," Sandy offered after introductions were made. It was funny to me that I was meeting people through my new neighbor instead of her meeting people through me.

After a short time of visiting, Sandy announced that it was time to begin. All settled down into a chair or couch and bowed their heads. One of the ladies prayed, asking the Lord to be with us and help us understand His Word. After the prayer she said, "We're in Philippians and will begin Colossians next week. Who would like to start?"

I leaned close to the lady sitting next to me and whispered, "What's a filipian and a colloshun?"

She whispered back, "They are small books in the New Testament."

"I guess I haven't gotten there yet. I've only read John and Acts and just started Romans," I quietly said, hoping not to disturb the others.

"Here, let me help you find them," the lady offered, much to my relief.

The others began discussing their assigned Bible reading. Each person read a portion of Scripture and commented on what it meant to her or how she applied it to her life. The group then made comments and suggestions, and asked or answered each other's questions.

The format of the Bible study was similar to that of the study group at my own house on Tuesday nights. The atmosphere here was totally different, however. As I listened to each lady speak, I tried to figure out why I felt a little charge of excitement bringing that fluttering feeling to my stomach. I heard nothing of significance up to this point, or at least that's what I thought. Actually the information was sailing over my head because of my lack of understanding. I watched each speaker with interest. One lady had a notebook with page after page of sentence diagrams. She had studied some verses so intently that she had broken the sentence structures down to better understand the meaning of the verses.

When the lady next to me finished, Priscilla said, "Mary, would you like to read a few verses for everyone to discuss?"

I knew Priscilla's intentions were not to put me on the spot but to help me feel included in the group. "Okay," I said. "What shall I read?"

"Read Philippians chapter four starting with verse one. You can read through verse nine," Priscilla instructed.

The obvious familiarity this group had with the Bible made me a little shaky, but I began with a clear voice. "Therefore, my brethren, dearly beloved and longed for, my joy and crown, so stand fast in the Lord, my dearly beloved. I beseech . . . uh . . . "

"Eu-o-dee-us," said my right-hand assistant.

"Euodias," I parroted. "Rejoice in the Lord alway . . . Be careful for nothing . . . let your requests be made known unto God. And the peace of God, which passeth all understanding . . . " I stopped cold. The words seemed to leap off the page at me. "Peace, peace, peace which passeth all understanding . . . peace, peace, peace which passeth all understanding. . . . "

I started shaking from head to foot. What's happening to me? These words are alive. How can this be? I don't understand. This has never happened with anything I've ever read before in my life. The thoughts crowded into my mind as I looked up from reading and into the faces around the room. They looked steady and comfortable. I could not continue reading.

"What is it, Mary? What's wrong?" someone asked.

I looked around at the faces again. I had no words to explain what was happening. Year after painful year, I had been on a search for peace that would rival a gold miner panning a huge river or digging with every ounce of strength to find a vein.

"And the peace of God, which passeth all understanding . . . " reverberated again through my mind. The words were like a living thing moving inside of me. Tears rushed to the rims of my eyes, and I was trying to choke back the power of emotion that was overwhelming me.

"Peace?" I said quietly to help keep my emotions controlled. "Peace that passes all understanding? Can I have *that* kind of peace?"

"Yes, Mary, you can," said Sandy. "It comes from knowing Jesus personally. Would you like to ask Him to come into your heart today?"

I had no idea what Sandy was talking about. "Ask Him into my heart? I don't know. I'll have to think about it. I think I'm going to go home now. Thank you for having me over." My words picked up speed as I became determined to leave. Someone brought Jeffery to me, and I managed to mumble goodbyes as I left for home.

That night I sat on the end of the sofa with my legs and feet curled up to keep warm. Dwayne and Keven were at their mom's house, Jennifer and Jeff were asleep, and Bob had gone to bed. The side arm of the sofa was high enough to make a great corner in which to nestle comfortably.

My Bible had a book marker at Romans chapter four, and I opened it quickly and began reading. I had only read four verses when again the words seemed to leap off the page and etch themselves into my mind and heart: "Now to him that worketh is the reward not reckoned of grace, but of debt. But to him that worketh not, but believeth on him that justifieth the ungodly, his faith is counted for righteousness."

The experience of a written word somehow moving into my being as a living thing engendered a hunger to read more and to have an understanding of what I was reading. I read the remainder of chapter four expectantly, but the words were just ink and paper. I went on to read chapter five.

"Therefore being justified by faith, we have peace . . . " There it is again, I thought to myself. There was no leaping effect this time, but the word "peace" caught my attention. "How, how?" I asked out loud to no one or perhaps to Someone whom I could not see.

" . . . with God through our Lord Jesus Christ," stated the rest of the verse. "Through our Lord Jesus Christ," I reiterated and then kept on with my reading.

"For when we were yet without strength, in due time Christ died for the ungodly." "Died for the ungodly," I pondered while I stared at verse six.

"But God commendeth his love toward us, in that, while we were yet sinners, Christ died for us," verse eight stated. Although these words were not leaping off the page, they were moving deep inside of my thoughts with a force that began to crack and break up boulders of philosophical input and humanistic theology.

Two chapters could not satisfy my spiritual appetite that night. I started reading chapter six like a hungry person unloading grocery bags in anticipation of a meal. I scanned the verses looking for that morsel of spiritual food and came to the last verse: "For the wages of sin is death; but the gift of God is eternal life through Jesus Christ our Lord."

"There it is; it's in verse twenty-three," I said to the inanimate air or to that invisible One for whom I had been searching so intensely to find.

As I closed the Bible I prayed, "Help me, God, help me to understand," this time purposely speaking to the One I could not see.

On Friday morning Sandy was at my door with a recipe she had written on a card. I welcomed her in and led her to the living room. "I'm so glad you came over, Sandy. I want to ask you more about Jesus coming into my heart. Would you pray with me?"

"Sure, Mary. It's simple: you just ask Him to forgive you of your sins and invite Him to come dwell in your heart and life. Tell the Lord that you want to live for Him."

"Would you pray first?" I asked her.

We sat on the couch and Sandy took my hand in hers. She began to pray out loud as I listened. When she finished I asked her, "What if I don't understand it very well; will He still come into my heart?"

"Yes," answered Sandy. "You have enough understanding to make a choice, Mary, and today you are choosing Jesus. You can rest assured that He sees your heart and will answer your prayer."

We bowed our heads and I began, "Jesus, You know I don't have a full understanding of this yet, but I want You to come into my heart. Please forgive me for my sins and teach me more about You. Thank You. Amen."

"He will teach you, Mary. The Bible says that His Spirit will lead you into truth. Keep reading His Word and the understanding will come. You also need to find a church to attend every Sunday."

"But how will I know which church to attend? The more I read in the Bible the more convinced I am that the churches Bob and I have been going to are not right in their teachings. I'm not familiar with the different denominations. How will I know which one's right?"

"I hope you will visit my church," Sandy said, "but I want to encourage you to pray. God will lead you to the right one for you and your family."

"I'm also going to pray about this group that meets in my house," I told Sandy. "Those people have been my friends for four years, and I can't treat them coldly."

Sandy arose to leave and said with confidence, "The Lord will help you handle that situation too."

For Mary—Gold Fever

Busy little miner,
Panning for that gold,
Digging here, searching there,
The main vein to unfold.

Hurray for Gold Fever!
You're on the right track,
But seek though you will,
You can't attain what you lack.

The gold is there,
And you know it's for you,
So go ask your Father;
He'll know what to do!

And whatever He tells you,
This you must do,
And He'll pan the gold,
As a reward for YOU!

For nothing is earned,
In the land of our Host.
It's all a free gift,
Lest any should boast!

Phyllis Buckner

Chapter Seven

Turning Point

The days passed rapidly like the turning pages of the Book in which I had become immersed, the Book that was like a living thing whose words could pierce the soul. Gradual changes were taking place in my life as the Word of the ages, the Bible, continued to transform my thinking. The daily intake of Scripture began to give me understanding and answers to my questions.

Sitting at the kitchen table, I thumbed back through the pages and looked at the underlined passages with the same excitement I felt when I had first seen them: "And be not conformed to this world: but be ye transformed by the renewing of your mind, that ye may prove what is that good, and acceptable, and perfect, will of God" (Romans 12:2). Yes, I'm being transformed, I thought. That is exactly what is happening as I read this Book. It is changing my life.

"For by grace are ye saved through faith; and that

not of yourselves: it is the gift of God: not of works, lest any man should boast'' (Ephesians 2:8-9). I thought about the night that I read that verse. It fit beautifully with the verses in Romans that I had not understood before. As I read Ephesians, I realized the meaning of the prayer Sandy had helped me to pray. It became clear to me that no amount of meditation and struggle to attain high levels of consciousness would bring the eternal peace my soul had ached to receive. If self-discipline alone warranted eternal life, then I might be able to boast over one with less discipline. By recognizing that a holy and righteous God took the death penalty for me while I was yet a sinner, I understood that I had no room to boast. God gets all the glory and rightfully so. Through a reference in the margin of my Bible I was directed to Isaiah and read, ''I am the LORD: that is my name: and my glory will I not give to another'' (Isaiah 42:8).

Heaven and hell were defined as states of consciousness in my old study group. Hell was taught to be the suffering we experience in this life that brings mental torment, and heaven was overcoming our difficulties and controlling our thoughts to bring peace, prosperity, and health. There was no teaching in the old study group about judgment or eternal punishment, but only of more chances to keep on trying to better oneself. The verses that I had marked in Matthew chapter twenty-five taught otherwise: ''And cast ye the unprofitable servant into outer darkness: there shall be weeping and gnashing of teeth. . . . And these shall go away into everlasting punishment: but the righteous into life eternal'' (Matthew 25:30, 46). ''Everlasting punishment'' gives no connotation of a second chance after death, and ''weeping and gnashing of teeth'' clearly describes a conscious torment rather than a state of oblivion.

The last book in the Bible, Revelation, described heaven to me as John, inspired by the Holy Ghost, wrote: "And God shall wipe away all tears from their eyes; and there shall be no more death, neither sorrow, nor crying, neither shall there be any more pain: for the former things are passed away. . . . And he shewed me a pure river of water of life, clear as crystal, proceeding out of the throne of God and of the Lamb. . . . And there shall be no night there; and they need no candle, neither light of the sun; for the Lord God giveth them light: and they shall reign for ever and ever'' (Revelation 21:4; 22:1, 5.) I read over the description again and yearned for that wonderful place, a place that really did exist and was not merely a state of mind.

Flipping through the pages of my Bible, I spotted another pencil marking and paused to reread Ephesians chapter four, verse twenty-nine: "Let no corrupt communication proceed out of your mouth, but that which is good to the use of edifying, that it may minister grace unto the hearers.'' I pictured my co-worker Linda from seven years earlier as she boldly stated, "Words are not right or wrong. They are only to express feelings.'' Linda's ideology had launched me into a verbal degradation that knew no bounds. Education was stilted in my life as the lazier road of four-letter words replaced an active pursuance of growth and learning. The Bible, God's Word, cut away the false ideology and set me free to become who God intended me to be.

A moment of reflection carried my thoughts back again to the mortgage company where I had worked.

Margaret! She was so quiet and unobtrusive. She remained untouched by her environment. In fact, now that I thought about it, she used to sit in the snack room and read a Bible during break time. She was a Christian, and I didn't have the eyes to see it. What was her last name? I wanted to call her and tell her of the changes happening in my life.

"Lord," I prayed, calling God by the title I had heard others use and now knowing Him well enough to use it myself, "I want to share with Margaret what You are doing in my life, but I can't remember her last name."

The name popped into my mind. "Thanks, Lord!" I said with amazement as I grabbed the phone book from the cabinet. Even in as big a city as Houston, there were only two families with her last name. I knew her husband's first name from those coffee-break conversations, so I was able to find the phone number.

I dialed Margaret's number with happy anticipation. A familiar voice answered the phone. "Margaret? This is Mary. We worked at the same company seven years ago. Do you remember me?" I queried.

"Yes, I do remember," Margaret responded with the surprise I expected to hear in her tone. "How are you?"

"Just fine! I called to tell you that I'm learning about the Lord. I remembered that you used to read the Bible on coffee breaks and that you were a steady person regardless of your surroundings. I'm just now understanding the kind of life you have been living and I'm so excited about it that I wanted to call and share my news with you," I blurted out to her.

"Well, that *is* good news, Mary. I'm glad for you," said Margaret.

"When I think about the way I was back then, Margaret, I'm ashamed," I said apprehensively. "As I look at those memories now, I can only imagine what you must have thought of me."

"But you're coming to know the Lord now, and that's what is important. You weren't so bad back then anyway," Margaret added in a comforting voice.

"Actually, I was, but thanks for the encouragement," I said.

"I have news for *you*," said Margaret in a way that denoted a change in the subject. "I am the mother of six-month-old twin boys. The Lord has blessed my husband and me with children of our own."

"Oh, that's great! The Lord is so good, and I'm finding out more all the time how good He is."

"Both of the babies are crying. It's time to feed them, Mary. I'll have to go now, but it was good to hear from you."

I hung up the phone and thanked the Lord for letting me clear up a piece of my past plus the bonus of hearing about the miracle He worked in Margaret's life. I was becoming increasingly aware that the loving kindness of God reached to the heavens. There was still a little time before Jeffery would wake up from his nap and Jennifer would be stepping off the schoolbus, so I went back to the table and continued feasting on God's Word.

Careful reading of the New Testament over a period of months made me familiar me with the order of the books that it contained, and I was now able to find specific portions of Scripture. I turned to the ninth chapter of Hebrews and reread verse twenty-seven: "And as it is appointed unto men once to die, but after this the judgment."

The night I had first read that verse was a landmark in time for me. The phrase "once to die, but after this the judgment" did more than just leap off the page at me; those words shot through my mind and spirit with the force of dynamite. When the smoke cleared, the concept of reincarnation had become shattered fragments that no man or book could ever reconstruct.

My first encounter with reincarnation and metaphysical philosophy occurred during my first marriage. Nine years had transpired with countless books building strength in those concepts until I had become ingrained with the doctrine of demons and the traditions of men. It took only one phrase from the Word of God to topple and destroy the years of false doctrine. The collected information from shelf upon shelf of books came tumbling down through the power of God's written Word. The Spirit of the living God moved through the words on the page, and my life was never the same again.

As I looked at the verse again, tears freely rolled down my cheeks. The probing, digging, teaching, correcting work of the Scriptures developed a tenderness in my heart that kept me filled up and spilling over with tears. I cried when I thought of God's mercy. I cried when I thought of His goodness. I cried when I thought of His power that was holding me, His wisdom that was teaching me, and His love that would never let me go.

"Thank You, Lord," I whispered to Him as I closed my Bible. "You are so great and so wonderful. Please teach me Your ways. Thank You for truth, and please give me understanding. I know now that reincarnation is wrong. It is a lie of the devil, the devil that I didn't even believe was real. You have shown me how real he is, Lord.

The devil is real, and he is a liar and the father of lies, a master deceiver. Lord, please explain to me how the devil can make lies like reincarnation so believable. How can scientists hypnotically regress a person's mind to describe past lives? How can an entranced person give details of towns and places in parts of the world where he or she has never been and then the details prove accurate? I don't understand that. I know enough, however, to realize that I can no longer be part of the study group. What are You going to do about that, Lord? They meet in my house and they're my friends. I'll leave that one with You for now. And, Lord, thanks that I can talk to You like a friend and come to You with all my questions."

The front door opened and Jennifer came in with a flourish saying, "Hi Mom! I'm home!"

From the end of the hallway, I could hear Jeff's voice. "Jeefer!" he called.

The activity level in the house accelerated as my quiet moment vanished. Jennifer grabbed her little brother in a bear hug. As Jeff squealed in jubilation at the attention he was getting, I peeled a banana for him and washed an apple for Jennifer.

While the children ate their snack, I got down to the serious business of plotting supper. This was no easy task at my house. Bob, being a full-blooded Yugoslavian, had different tastes from mine. He was bringing Dwayne and Keven over that night and they, being half Yugoslavian and the other half Yankee, did not have an appreciation for my Southern belle cooking.

I tapped my fingers on the kitchen counter as I contemplated what to cook. My reputation as the casserole queen was of no help to these males who wanted a distinct separation of each food category on their plates. Meal planning was further complicated by a variety of allergies in the family. Jennifer's milk allergy eliminated cooking with all milk products including cheeses, creamed soups, and canned goods that contained whey or milk solids. Dwayne's mother kept a close watch on his meals in an attempt to alleviate his frequent asthma attacks.

This is a case for prayer, I decided. "Lord, what do You suggest? These Yugoslavians love pasta, but I am spaghettied out."

Salisbury steaks came to my mind. "Hmm," I thought. "That will work. With a few substitutions, I can make it milk free. Some gravy on top and mashed potatoes, peas, and a salad on the side will make it a meal. Thanks again, Lord."

Dinner was ready when Bob came in with the boys. Bob went to take off his tie and put away his briefcase. Dwayne and Keven were empty-handed: they kept a supply of clothes at our house because of the frequency and length of their stays. The boys went to wash their hands while I called Jennifer and Jeffery. When everyone was ready, we gathered around the table.

As an active child, Jennifer was always ready to eat. "Mom, this looks good," she enthusiastically noted.

"Food always looks good to you, Jennifer. It's these other guys I'm working on. Look, fellows, the peas are over here and the potatoes are over there," I remarked with a sense of accomplishment.

"This is it; we like it," responded the Yugoslavian contingent.

"Thank You, Lord," I sighed.

"Why do you say that?" asked Bob.

"This is nothing short of a victory," I told him. "Meal planning around here is like walking through a minefield: one wrong move and—BLAM!—a war of nations or sick children. But I asked the Lord for help. I'm finding out that I can go to God for everything I need."

"You're changing, Mary," Bob commented.

"I know," I responded. "It's the Bible that is changing me. I've been reading it every night for a while now. In fact, there is something I would like to talk to you about after supper, okay?"

Our peaceful meal of categorized foods ended, and the three older children helped me with K.P. duty. Keven always had an urgent restroom excuse when dish washing was mentioned. I had to chuckle as I remembered my younger sister used to pull that same trick while my older sister, Carol, washed dishes and I dried them and put them away. Keven reappeared in time to wipe the table and counter tops.

Dwayne, Keven, and Jennifer bolted out the door to run and play before dark. Bob and I sat in the living room to talk while Jeffery entertained himself with some toys on the floor.

"Bob, I want to talk to you about church," I began cautiously. "In reading the Bible, I've come to understand some things about God. I realize now that the church we have been going to does not agree with the teachings in the Bible. I am no longer able to keep going to that church."

"Not able . . . what do you mean, Mary?"

"It's something very strong inside of me. As I read the New Testament, I saw some things that I never knew before. I see now that we are not all at one with God, but that we are sinners who deserve death and Jesus died for us. I can't stay in that church anymore, Bob. I have to find a church that agrees with the Bible."

"I don't see it, though, Mary. I'm not ready to change churches, and I don't want our family split up on Sundays. We need to stay together."

"I agree. I want very much to keep the family together. It's one of the most important things in life to me. But there is one thing, only one, more important, and that is God Himself. Bob, even you, as close as you are to me, may not realize the extent of searching I've gone through for the past nine years. Finally, I am getting answers. I am getting to know God in a way that I never knew Him. There is no way I can turn back. I have a proposal for you," I said slowly and quietly. "I propose," I continued, "that we find a church together where we can all be happy."

"How?" asked Bob.

"Well, I read in the Bible that a wife is to submit to her husband. I want to do that, Bob. That means you *are* the head of the house. I cannot take up the leadership, especially the spiritual leadership, even if I wanted to take it. It's not mine to take according to God's Word. I can, however, make a proposal to you for your consideration. Bob, there are many churches, so there has to be a place where we can go together. I think if we ask God to help us that He will lead us where to go."

"What if I want to stay where we are?" asked Bob.

"That I can't do."

"It doesn't sound to me like you're submitting."

"There is a line, Bob," I responded.

"A line. What line?" he asked in his even-tempered way.

"Bob, the scriptural disagreements that I see with that church are strong. I want to submit to you and will in everything except one case. That is, when it directly contradicts the Bible. In that case I must go with the Bible. I must, Bob," I restated for emphasis but in a calm tone.

This was a difficult conversation. I mentally sent up a fervent prayer, "Lord, please help me right now. Help me. I need You right now. Give me a quiet spirit and wisdom, please."

"Bob," I started again, "I want our family to be together just as much as you do. I cannot explain it to you any better than this: deep inside of me, the Word of God has penetrated my soul or spirit or something. I only know that the church we've been attending is wrong, and I can never go back there again. I can never go back."

"Well, Mary, I don't see how you can call this submission, and I'm not ready to change churches right now."

Darkness had descended, and three youngsters reappeared in the house. The discussion was closed for the night. I took Jeffery's hand and directed him to the bathtub where I busily scrubbed him down. I knew Bob well enough to know that he would take time to think through everything. He was not about to make a change based on what he thought might be a female whim. I felt pressure and emotional pain as I waited through his thinking process. It was not until years later that I learned to greatly appreciate the slow-moving, careful deliberation that was my husband's habit in making decisions.

Chapter Eight

A Place to Worship

Sunday morning arrived. No words were exchanged, but somehow the message had passed between me and Bob that we would be staying home that day. We slept later than usual and let the children sleep too.

Jennifer was the first one up. She was always the first one to go to bed and often the first one to awaken. The family still laughs about the time Jennifer fell asleep in her plate at the supper table when she was five years old. Sitting straight up in her chair, she slowly began to lean forward. At first we didn't realize that she had fallen fast asleep. Her head went lower and lower until her face was resting on the remaining food on her plate. I had to wake her up gently, clean her face, and put her to bed.

Jennifer had us all beat when it came to mornings, though. She always woke up bright and cheery and ready for the day. It was not surprising that Jennifer was the first one up that Sunday morning. I heard her little rustlings and knew it was time for me to get up too. Dwayne and Keven were pancake lovers, and I decided this would be a good day to make a lot of pancakes.

The delectable aroma wafted down the hall, and before too long, three boys and a dad were filling up the kitchen.

"Jennifer, you'd better come quick," I called to her. "The guys are in here with forks in hands."

Jennifer rounded the corner in time to get her share of breakfast. There were plenty of pancakes, and when we pushed away from the table, we each had that heavy feeling for which pancakes are famous. We retired to the living room to read the Sunday comics and newspaper.

It didn't take long before the children were through with their reading and migrated to the back bedroom. One of their favorite pastimes was building an indoor fort using the boys' bunk beds as the framework. Blankets were hung over and around the beds and then secured with clothespins. Chairs and other smaller pieces of furniture were used with additional blankets to extend the fort out into the spacious room. These forts were quite elaborate and easily accommodated all four children. This would occupy them for hours.

While Bob remained behind the newspaper and assorted sizes of children scurried through the house collecting clothespins and blankets, I took the opportunity of having time to myself. In the front bedroom with the door closed, I knelt beside the bed and prayed. "Lord, thank You for Your Word. Thank You for opening my eyes to Your Word that I may learn of You. You know that I want to go to church and worship You. You see my family and my husband. I bring Bob to You right now and ask that You would open his eyes too. We don't know what church to go to. Please help us find a place that teaches according to Your Word. In Jesus' name, amen."

For two or three weeks, we did not go to church. One evening during that time Bob talked to me about going back to the church we had been attending. I answered him calmly and unwaveringly. "No, Bob. I can't. Under no conditions will I go back to that church. Pick a church that agrees with God's Word and I will go with you. You choose for us, and we'll all go together."

"How can I choose for us? You seem to be the one making the choices," Bob countered.

"I told you, Bob, there is a line. Anything on the other side of the line, the side that disagrees with the Bible, I can't be a part of. Anything on this side of the line, the side that lines up with God's Word, is in the proverbial hat from which to choose. There is a whole array of churches that we can visit. Where would you like to go first?"

It was enough at that time to refuse a church with false doctrine. Quiet, unwavering refusal to return to our previous church spoke volumes to my husband. Adding demands to the firm refusal would have distanced him further from me and from God's Word. God gave me the wisdom to know that I could not choose the next church and demand our family's attendance. By asking Bob where he would like to go next, he was thrust into the leadership position intended by God. Asking Bob where he would like the family to go next caught him off guard. He was expecting arguments, but instead he was met with quiet refusals and new options that evidenced I would follow his lead.

When a wife steps back and lets her husband take the lead, he may test her. In my early walk with God, Bob did not always make the decisions that I wanted him to make. The Lord taught me to be quiet and submit—no matter what—as long as the decision was not sinful or did not contradict the Bible. I would present my case to my husband and leave the final decision to him.

More than once, Bob's final decision went against my wishes. Sometimes his decision caused me great emotional pain. I continually took my hurts to God in prayer and poured my heart out to Him. The Lord gave me the calmness, which is definitely not my character, and the strength to submit even when it hurt.

One time Bob announced a decision that he had made concerning a particular situation and I just stood and looked at him. Tears ran silently down my cheeks and I said, "You have heard my opinions and thinking on the matter, and this is what you have decided. It is totally against my feelings and wishes, and you know that. I just want to tell you—I'm behind you one hundred percent. This is what you have decided, and this is what we'll do."

After those words, I left the room and went to the bedroom. I knelt by the bed and cried quietly. Bob came into the room and sat on the bed near me. He put his hand on my shoulder and began to comfort me. "Mary, I really need to do this," he said. "Thanks for standing with me."

From that day forward, my husband took my feelings into consideration very seriously. He saw that I would indeed submit to him even to my own hurt. Responsibility pressed on his shoulders as he realized that his decisions would radically affect his family because we were following his lead. Each decision became important to him; he knew his decisions were being taken seriously.

Bob reconsidered my first question of where to take the family to church. The following Sunday Bob told us to put on our church clothes. "Where are we going?" I asked.

"I'm not sure," Bob said. "Let's get in the car and ask God where to go."

"Well, that's innovative," I said. "I'm for it. Let's go."

As we backed out of the driveway, we took turns naming the churches in the area. Bob picked a Protestant church of a major denomination and even asked me what I thought about it. "We just need one that teaches that Jesus died for our sins and that doesn't teach reincarnation, Bob. That's all I know. Let's go check it out."

We arrived early enough at the church to get an empty pew. With six in our family, we almost filled an entire row on one side of the sanctuary. We eyed our surroundings and surveyed the other people arriving for the service. The room would accommodate about two hundred people and was quickly filling up. Sunlight streamed in through the long, narrow windows lining the outer walls. A large wooden cross was affixed to the front wall. The pulpit and choir chairs were on a raised platform under the cross.

The choir director walked to the pulpit and began a congregational song. Bob and I found the song in the hymnal so that we could follow along with it. I listened carefully through the first verse and chorus to catch on to the melody, and then I joined in with the singing. "Just as I am without one plea . . . ," I sang with everyone.

As we continued through the verses and the chorus, I was touched to the core by the words of the song. " . . . but that Thy blood was shed for me . . . and that Thou bidst me come to thee, O Lamb of God, I come. . . . "

"I come . . . ," I repeated and my heart leaped inside of me. Tears again coursed down my face. I looked briefly around and saw only sober faces and dry eyes.

"Lord, I don't know why I'm always crying. I've never seen anybody cry so much. It's just that something wells up so big inside that I can't keep it in. To think that You take me just as I am, Lord, that's enough to make me cry. I tried so hard to climb up to You and now I find out that You reached down to me."

The choir director took a seat, and a small, dark-haired man in his late twenties or early thirties stepped up to the pulpit. He read a verse of Scripture and began to talk about it in a conversational voice. I glanced at Bob to see if he was interested in the sermon. The soft-spoken minister had Bob's complete attention.

"Oh good!" I muttered to myself. "He's listening. And from what I'm hearing, it sounds like this man is preaching according to the Bible. Now Bob will hear the Word too. Oh, thank You, Lord."

The sermon lasted only twenty minutes. As people were leaving and others were visiting, the pastor and his wife came to me and Bob. I could tell that my husband immediately liked this young man. We chatted with them for a few minutes, and they invited us to come back.

Bob was quiet as we rode home, so I ventured to ask him, "What did you think about the church?"

"I liked it," he said. "I especially liked that minister. He seems like a nice guy. He's quiet and even-tempered."

"Just like you," I said with a smile. "I liked it too, and best of all, it lines up with what I've read in the Bible as far as I can tell."

"I wouldn't mind going there again," Bob said.

We had found a place to worship together as a family. That afternoon I took time to get on my knees and thank God for His hand in my life and in my family.

I had several things to thank the Lord for that day. The old study group had not only quit meeting at our house but had disbanded altogether. The national organization was still viable, but the people in our local group suddenly scattered.

The people who made up the core of that local group had been together for ten to twelve years. I was one of the later members who joined them. The regularity of the group's attendance over such a long period of time clearly showed that God's hand was in the dispersion of it. It was not chance or coincidence that every member withdrew from the group in the same week. Some of them moved. Other members remained in the area, but they never met together again.

There is no doubt in my mind that the disbanding of that group was a direct answer to prayer. It was an act of a heavenly Father taking care of one who was feeding on the milk of His Word. He did it for me.

The next thing I thanked God for was the understanding He gave me of the dream I had before I had met Mardel. The answer came again through the written Word of God. I read: "And I saw heaven opened, and behold a white horse; and he that sat upon him was called Faithful and True, and in righteousness he doth judge and make war. His eyes were as a flame of fire, and on his head were many crowns; and he had a name written, that no man knew, but he himself. And he was clothed with a vesture dipped in blood: and his name is called The Word of God" (Revelation 19:11-13).

When I had prayed asking God to come find me because I could not find Him, it moved the heart of God. Before the week was over, I had the dream in which a choice was set before me. The white horse was on one side of the room, and the study group was in the other direction. I closed the door of the room, shutting out the group. At that moment the white horse leaped through the window and killed me.

In Revelation, the One who is called the Word of God rode upon the white horse. Closing out the study group in my life opened the window to the Word of God. As I nightly read the Scriptures, the false doctrine I had accumulated was destroyed or killed. The Word of God had the power to annihilate even the deeply ingrained lies.

What a mighty God we serve! He is a prayer-answering God. He will move heaven and earth to bring truth to a soul. He *is* truth, and He gave His life so that whosoever believes in Him should not perish but have everlasting life (John 3:16; 14:6).

The Lord said through the prophet Jeremiah, "And ye shall seek me, and find me, when ye shall search for me with all your heart" (Jeremiah 29:13). I sought God with all my heart. When I gave up my own ways and asked Him to come to me, He moved faster than I could comprehend. As I began to respond to His written Word, the understanding began to come.

I had walked a long road of error and sin after that first spontaneous prayer in the red-carpeted apartment.

God never took His eyes off me for one minute. He knew exactly how to order the circumstances in my life to answer that first prayer. Six years passed while I tried everything humanity had to offer. God patiently waited for me to run out of places to look until in desperation I looked up to Him. He had answered my first prayer. I knelt before Him with astonishment as I looked at His work in my life.

Before I arose from this prayer of thanksgiving, I asked two things of the Lord: (1) that He would cleanse my mind of the shattered pieces of false doctrine and (2) that He would give me understanding of how the devil can perpetrate the lies I had believed.

Chapter Nine

Answers

The boys' quarters, otherwise known as the master bedroom, was well suited to three growing, energetic youngsters. The familiar sound of a ruckus coming from that direction drew me to the hallway.

Anger poured adrenalin into my central nervous system, moving my feet rapidly down the hall. Why do I have to be the one to take care of this? I thought, adding frustration to my anger. Bob is always out in those flower beds when Dwayne and Keven fight and fuss. Then he shows up when it's all over and thinks that I am some kind of ogre. Anyway, what am I going to do to those boys? I don't know how to handle this.

I stopped suddenly halfway down the hall. That's a good question. What *am* I going to do when I reach the bedroom? I never seem to handle these situations right.

A verse of Scripture popped into my mind: "If any of you lack wisdom, let him ask of God, that giveth to all men liberally, and upbraideth not; and it shall be given him'' (James 1:5).

What an idea! I'll ask the *Lord* what to do.

"Lord, please tell me what to do with the boys. It sounds pretty wild in their bedroom, Lord, but I'm not budging from here until I hear from You,'' I said with a tone of finality depicting trust.

A feeling of calmness and peace descended upon me. The frustration and anger melted away. I walked the remaining length of the hall with even-paced and purposeful steps. Entering the bedroom, I was surprised to hear my voice speaking in a firm and controlled tone issuing clear directives to the pair of young brawlers.

Putting a hand on the shoulder of each boy, I looked straight into their faces and commanded the arguing to stop as I firmly pulled them apart. I kept my hand on their shoulders as both Dwayne and Keven looked up at me. With my right hand I directed Dwayne over to the bed. "You sit right there until further notice,'' I instructed.

"Keven, come with me,'' I ordered. My voice strongly implied that he had no choice. With my left hand still on Keven's shoulder, I ushered him into Jennifer's room and seated him on her bed. "Stay right there until I come back.''

I closed the bedroom doors and went back to the living room, marveling at what had just transpired. Past scenes of power struggles played before my eyes. I saw myself yelling at Dwayne or Keven and heard their argumentative responses. The discipline of stepchildren is sensitive. The children know it, and all sets of parents know it. Frustration and anger stem from fear of the natural parent's reactions to the stepparent's discipline. This leads the stepparent to feel helpless to control the children. To make matters worse, the natural parent often hesitates to discipline his own children due to thoughts such as, "I only have them for a few days. I can't spend the time always correcting them."

How different the scene was this time. Reflecting on the event, I knew it wasn't what I did that made the difference; it was the way I did it. I was in complete control. I knew it and the boys knew it.

I sat down in the blue high-backed rocker. The triple window that filled most of the front wall offered a view of the entire courtyard. I could see Bob trimming the top of a row of bushes that formed a neat hedge beside the outer wall of the master bedroom.

"We did it," I said toward the window as if Bob could hear me. "The Lord and I, we did it right. Thank You, Jesus."

A series of instructive thoughts began to fill my mind: learn to respond instead of react to people and circumstances around you, be slow to speak, do not make empty threats, predetermine disciplinary action, and follow through. "Lord, this is incredible. I can come to You with *everything*. You are so good! I can't thank You enough. You are truly there in my time of need."

Prayer was becoming a lifestyle to me. The more I prayed, the more God answered and moved in my life. It became obvious to me that praying was the smart thing to do. But it was more than that. Prayer was a lifeline to One I was growing to love more every day.

I learned more about prayer at the new church we had been attending. The ladies quickly befriended me, and I soaked in their conversation and tutelage from their years of Christian experience.

Two ladies in particular attracted my attention because of their love for the Bible and prayer. One of them was named Marge. There was nothing flashy about her; she was plain-faced and dressed in simple attire. Marge was always the first one to suggest prayer, and her methodical lifestyle illustrated her stability and faithfulness. Judy was a petite redhead who epitomized the image of clean and neat.

Marge, Judy, and I began meeting every Wednesday morning to pray. We took turns meeting in each other's homes, praying for our families, our church, our friends, and our country.

Marge perceived how quickly I was learning, and one day she said, "I want to take you to meet someone, Mary. It's a very special lady who knows the Bible so well that many people go to her for godly counsel. She prays a lot too, and I think she will be just as glad to meet you. Her name is Ruth. She spends each weekday in a room at her church and trusts the Lord for her subsistence."

This description of Ruth was very interesting to me, and I was eager to meet her. Marge picked me up later in the week, and we went to the large church in the middle of town. Five or six cars of church staff occupied the otherwise empty parking lot. Marge parked at the front end of the building, and we opened our car doors to the heat of the brilliant summer day. I followed Marge around the sidewalk to the first door.

Ruth opened the door as we reached the threshold. "Come in, come in. I've been expecting you, Marge. And this must be Mary," she said, looking up at me.

What a big smile on this little woman, I thought to myself. It was easy to warm up to Ruth. Even the small wrinkles around her blue eyes hinted that smiles were a habit for this lady. Her light-colored hair obfuscated any gray and softened the early signs of aging in her features. Since I stood head and shoulders above her, she must have been barely over five feet tall.

Ruth motioned to some metal folding chairs, and we each took a seat. A nearby table was filled with books, pamphlets, and tracts. Tiered display racks housed more literature around the room.

"So, Mary, tell me about yourself," invited Ruth.

"Oh! You jump right in, unlike most people. I don't know where to start. You've caught me off guard, Ruth."

"That's okay. Just take your time," Ruth encouraged.

"I haven't known the Lord very long, and I have a lot to learn. My husband and I were involved with the occult, but we have come to understand that metaphysics is not God's way. Bob and I were trying to attain perfection through our own good works, the power of positive thinking, and visualizing the way we wanted things to be. The funny thing is that our efforts never produced the desired outcome. I didn't see a change in my life until I accepted Jesus as my Savior and started reading the Bible instead of just looking at Scripture out of context. Bob goes to church with me, but he hasn't accepted Jesus yet."

"Mary, you have been involved in something we call humanism," Ruth explained.

"Then you know what I'm talking about. What a relief! The Christians I've met so far don't understand my words and can't answer some of my questions. The good news is that Jesus understands my questions and has been answering me as I read the Bible every day."

"That's beautiful, Mary. By turning to Jesus and His

written Word, you will learn quickly. Don't be surprised if you begin to pass up people who have been in the church all of their lives."

"How can that happen? It doesn't look to me that I can even catch up to them much less pass them up."

"Many people go to church on Sunday and forget God the rest of the week, Mary. His Word is 'quick and powerful.' If you continue to read it every day you will 'grow in grace, and in the knowledge of our Lord and Saviour Jesus Christ.' "

Ruth's words were captivating. I didn't realize at the time that Scripture was interwoven with her own words, providing a power beyond herself.

"I want to caution you, Mary. You must keep a right spirit. Never look down on others. To whom much is given, much is required."

"Ruth, I don't understand what you are saying."

She smiled at me. "One day you will, and I pray that the Lord will then bring these words back to you. God is love and full of mercy and compassion. He who has been forgiven much must always remember to forgive others. Learn to be patient with people, and don't become their judge. God alone is the judge."

Now I was crying. Ruth hit that tender spot inside of me. "I have been forgiven so much. I remember reading that while I was yet a sinner, Christ died for me. I can hardly contain it, Ruth. I have never known a love like this before. I'm praying for my husband. I want him to know Jesus like this too."

"That's good, Mary. Prayer is the answer. God moves through the prayers of His people. There are some specific prayers you need to pray since you were involved with the occult. You need to renounce that involvement. Were you involved with astrology and mediums?"

"Yes. I read many things about people who went into trances and information flowed through them. I believed those things. Also, I went to a woman who read my astrological chart and told me many things about myself that were accurate. I have used tarot cards lots of times. I was into transcendental meditation and so much more that I couldn't tell it all in one visit."

"Were you involved with drugs too?" Ruth asked.

"Grass," I answered.

"Mary, all sin is sin, but you have opened doors to the spirit realm through drugs and the occult. These doors need to be closed through prayer. Will you renounce these things before the Lord?"

"Oh, yes, yes," I said through another flood of tears.

"I can see that you do. That's good, because it must come from your heart. It's very simple, Mary. Just tell the Lord you renounce each of these things you were involved with. Ask His forgiveness. The blood He shed on the cross is powerful enough to cleanse you from all sin. Then you must never pick these things up again. Stay away from all of it."

Ruth handed me a small paper that contained the instructions she had given me. "Take this home and read it to help you understand it better. You can pray at home, because it's Jesus you need to talk to about these things, not me. There is only one mediator between God and man, the man Christ Jesus."

"Thank you," I said as I clutched the paper in my lap.

"You also need to know about spiritual weapons," Ruth continued. "Let me show you a portion of Scripture in Ephesians."

Opening the Bible that lay near her on the table, Ruth read: "Put on the whole armour of God, that ye may be able to stand against the wiles of the devil. For we wrestle not against flesh and blood, but against principalities, against powers, against the rulers of the darkness of this world, against spiritual wickedness in high places" (Ephesians 6:11-12).

"Ruth, look!" I exclaimed. "Rulers of the darkness of this world—that's how he does it!"

"Who does what, Mary?"

"The devil. I didn't even believe in an actual devil, but now I know he really exists. He's not just an evil force either; he's a real being. I asked God to show me how the devil deceives people into believing all of that metaphysical stuff. The devil can't be in every place at once like God. He evidently has a network of cohorts."

"That's right. Let me show you another passage of Scripture. It's Deuteronomy 18:10-12. 'There shall not be found among you any one that maketh his son or his daughter to pass through the fire, or that useth divination, or an observer of times, or an enchanter, or a witch, or a charmer, or a consulter with familiar spirits, or a wizard, or a necromancer. For all that do these things are an abomination unto the LORD; and because of these abominations the LORD thy God doth drive them out from before thee.' "

"Divination—that would mean things like astrology and tarot cards. What's a necromancer?" I inquired.

"That means communicating with the dead. You see, Mary, when people think they are communicating with their loved ones, they are really being deceived."

"Ruth, that's cruel. How can God be so cruel?"

"No, Mary. God is not cruel. The devil is cruel. Anyone who loves God enough to read His Word can discover that we cannot communicate with the dead or work through familiar spirits."

"What are familiar spirits?" I asked.

"That's what you were reading about in these people who go into trances. That's why they have a degree of accuracy. The devil and his demons, or cohorts as you said, have enough accuracy that people who don't know the Bible can be duped or deceived."

"But, Ruth, how come I read of so many *good* things done through these mediums? For example, many people found answers to their health problems through these mediums. I was so drawn to that because I seem to be getting weaker and sicker. I miss the health I enjoyed as a child and a teenager."

"The devil is subtle. If he shows his true colors, not many people would succumb to his evil ways. The Bible says that Satan can produce lying wonders, transform himself into an angel of light, and blind the minds of those who do not believe. The wretched evil behind his schemes is often camouflaged behind a facade of good. If something is an abomination to God, it is *not* good, no matter how good it looks."

"Ruth! This answers one of my major questions. Satan can produce lying wonders, and he has an army of demons who give information through people that make themselves available for them. That explains how descriptions can be given of places where a person has never been."

"What do you mean, Mary?"

"Reincarnation—I found out from the Bible that it

is a lie, but I couldn't understand how the devil pulled it off," I answered.

Marge had been sitting quietly during all of this. I looked at her and said, "God used you to bring me here today. I asked God to explain these things to me, and He is answering my prayer."

"I didn't understand your questions either, Mary, but I was hoping Ruth could help you. It's hard for us who have been in the church all of our lives to understand where you are coming from. Ruth knows the Bible so well that I thought she would have some answers for you."

"Before you get away, I still want to talk to you about weapons," interjected Ruth. "The weapons of our warfare are not carnal, but mighty to the pulling down of strongholds. All of the armor mentioned in Ephesians is defensive. Then one offensive weapon is named. It is the sword of the Spirit, the Word of God. Learn to pray the Word. Look at Philippians 1:9-11. I would pray this for you, Mary: 'that your love may abound yet more and more in knowledge and in all judgment; that ye may approve things that are excellent; that ye may be sincere and without offence till the day of Christ; being filled with the fruits of righteousness, which are by Jesus Christ, unto the glory and praise of God.' "

"That's wonderful! I'm going to do that for others," I decided out loud. "Are there more places like that in the Bible?"

"Yes, you will find them as you read, but you will also learn to incorporate appropriate verses into your prayers and conversation. The power is in *His* Word, not yours. That's why I teach people to be in the Word and have the Word in them. Learn also to call on the name of the

Lord. His name is 'a strong tower'; the righteous can run into it and are safe. When you feel afraid, call on Jesus. When you are troubled, call on Jesus. His name is a strong tower. Mary, pray for your husband and family by using the Word and the name of Jesus. Pull down strongholds and bind the enemy in the spirit realm with the powerful and lovely name of Jesus. Every knee must bow to the name of Jesus."

I could have sat there all day. I was hungrily feasting on the words flowing from Ruth. It wasn't until later that I discovered it was because of all of the Scripture interspersed throughout her conversation. I wasn't feasting on Ruth's words. She was feeding me the Word of God.

Ruth put a second pamphlet in my hand. It was about battling the devil in prayer and contained the things Ruth had been discussing.

"Before you leave, I would like the three of us to pray together," requested Ruth.

We bowed our heads, and Ruth asked the Lord to teach me and lead me. She asked Him to save my family and protect me from the powers of darkness.

Ruth gave Marge and me each a parting hug and told me to come see her anytime. As Marge and I stepped back into the sunlight, I was oblivious to the burning heat of summer.

"I've never known anyone like her, Marge. I'm awed. She helped me so much. She knew the Bible. I want to be like that. Do you think I could ever be like that? I want to help people."

Marge was laughing. "Mary, you get so excited that it's funny. Calm down and be patient. God isn't finished with you yet, and Rome wasn't built in a day."

Now I was laughing. "Marge, you're funny too. You're so calm all the time. I've never seen your feathers ruffled. Maybe that's why we're good friends. I intensify everything, and you calm it all back down."

"I suspected you and Ruth would click," Marge said.

"Thanks for bringing me to her. Now I've got to learn more about this warfare she talked about. I have a family to pray for."

In Search of Light

Desolate wasteland, dark and dry,
Oppressive night of the serpent's lie,
Hinder not my soul to rise,
Pressing up to the morning skies!

Oh bright Morning Star,
Illuminate my soul!
Fill me with light.
I long for the light;
This night is so long for my soul!

Oh majestic Wonder!
How precious each moment
When, for a moment,
My soul is bathed in wonder.

Each glimmer of understanding,
Precious gems of understanding,
Weeping, my soul cries for more.

Glory! Splendor!
The night cannot hinder!
On the wings of the morning I'll soar!

Phyllis Buckner

Chapter Ten

Storming the Gates of Hell

"I bind you, Satan, in the name of the Lord Jesus Christ. Let go of my family in Jesus' name. I renounce any ties you have in me and my family through the occult, drugs, promiscuity, and divorces." Kneeling on the bedroom floor I spoke forcefully, confident of the power in the name of the One who has all power in heaven and on earth.

Lifting my face upward, I redirected my attention. "Lord Jesus, I bring my husband and children to You. Please open their eyes that they may come to know You in truth."

The next day, while Jeff took a nap, I went again to the bedroom and got on my knees. "Devil, you let go of my family in Jesus' name! Lord Jesus, save my family! Open my husband's eyes. Do a work in his heart, Lord. Let him see his need of You."

The next day I was in the bedroom again. "Satan, you must loose your hold on my family! I pull down the lies and deceit you have used to blind us. You no longer have power over me, my husband, and our children. The Bible says where one in the household is saved, the whole house is sanctified. You have no part in my family now, devil."

Looking upward I prayed, "Lord Jesus, open my husband's eyes. I praise You, Jesus. With You all things are possible. There is nothing too hard for You, Lord."

On Saturday the house was full of activity with the family at home. I went into the closet to pray. "Lord, here I am in the closet. Your Word says to pray in our closets in secret. Whether You meant that literally or not, I don't know, but today it sure is a great idea. Lord, save my family. Bring them to a knowledge of the truth. *You are truth, Lord*! You said that You are the way, the truth, and the life. I bring my family to *You*, Jesus. When they find You, they will find truth. I praise Your name, Jesus. You are worthy to be praised."

On Sunday morning our whole family went to church. Seated beside Bob, I silently prayed, "Lord, show Bob the truth about mind control. Show him the truth about ESP, holistic healing, positive thinking, and that lie about the divine presence within. Show him that it's *You*, Lord, that You are *real*. Let him see that You alone are God, that You are the Creator, and that we are not one and the same with You but that we are Your creation. Show him, Lord, that the devil has people worshiping the creature of self more than You, the Creator. Give him understanding, Lord. And, Jesus, I just want to tell You that I love You."

The next day I prayed and the next and the next and the next. I prayed week after week, and then the weeks turned into months. On Wednesdays I met with Marge and Judy to bind together with them in prayer.

One day I called Marge and said, "I was just reading Acts 19:18-20. It says: 'And many that believed came, and confessed, and shewed their deeds. Many of them also which used curious arts brought their books together, and burned them before all men: and they counted the price of them, and found it fifty thousand pieces of silver. So mightily grew the word of God and prevailed.' Marge, did you catch what happened in those verses? They destroyed their curious arts. That means their idols and ungodly items. They burned their ungodly books and didn't even consider it a financial loss. When they were clean before the Lord, the Word of God prevailed. I want God's Word to prevail at my house. I have plenty of things from my past. Will you come over for a book burning and a prayer meeting?"

"Sure, Mary. I would be glad to. When should I come?"

"Can you come tomorrow afternoon? We can pray while Jeff takes his nap and Jennifer is at school."

"Okay, that will be fine," said Marge. "I'll see you tomorrow."

Jeffery was already asleep in the back bedroom when Marge knocked on the door. She was full of questions as she entered the house. "What have you got in mind, Mary? Are we going to burn something? I've never done this before. How will we do it? This is sure different."

"I've never done anything like this before either, Marge. I would never have thought of it myself. I just saw it in the Bible. I've been praying every day for my family and now I see the importance of having a clean house before God. He is a jealous God and will have no gods before Him. I'm showing the devil and the Lord how serious I am. I want no part of those things I was involved with before I knew Jesus."

"So what do you have, Mary?" Marge asked with slight trepidation.

"Books! I have boxes full of books from the occult. In addition to the Book of Acts, I read in Kings and Chronicles about God's people forsaking Him to serve idols. When they turned back to God, they destroyed the groves, idols, and anything that was an abomination to the Lord. They cleaned up!" I stated emphatically.

"I'm ready," said Marge. "How are we going to do this?"

"In the fireplace, of course. I've boxed up the books from the bedroom shelves. I only took down mine, though. I didn't touch Bob's. Since God put husbands over the house I think we need to leave Bob's things alone. Let's let God deal with him. I think that by doing my part, the Lord will see that I truly have chosen Him above all else. From what I've read in the Bible, God honors things like that, and I can leave the rest to Him."

"These boxes are too heavy for us, Mary," Marge said as she eyed the brimming contents of the two boxes on the floor.

"I know. We can take armfuls, or we can try to push the boxes. Let's try pushing first."

Marge pushed from one side of a box while I pulled. "OOPS! My back! This won't work, Marge. My lower back can't take it. It will go out, and I'll be stuck on the floor. I've had that happen many times. It's so excruciating that I don't want to risk it. Let's take armloads."

I knelt beside the box. Gathering as many books as I could carry in the crook of my left arm, I pushed up from the floor with my right arm, being careful to keep my back straight. Marge was already making a trip to the fireplace. We crossed paths as she made her way back to the bedroom and I went to the fireplace.

"You *do* have a lot of these, Mary. Where did you get so many?" Marge asked as she blazed a trail from the bedroom to the living room.

"It's just that I was reading them for years and they accumulated," I told her. "Marge, do you know how to start a fire?"

"You're kidding, right?" Marge asked with a look of unbelief on her face.

"No, really. I've never started a fire. Now that I think about it, I don't know how. We can't use the fireplace that much because of all the allergies among us. The logs make us cough and sneeze and our eyes swell. When we do have a fire, Bob makes it."

"Well, I'm not overly informed on it either," said Marge, "but I think I know enough to accomplish our task today."

"I know about the flue," I offered, hoping to encourage Marge with our endeavor. "We have to pull this chain to open up the chimney. These two small logs in here should be sufficient. We just need enough wood and paper to start it up. I have some long matches too."

"It sounds to me like you know more about it than you realize," said Marge.

"I must have picked up a little bit from watching Bob."

"Between the two of us, we're going to make it," she

responded. "Get some paper to tear up for tinder."

"Tinder? That's good, Marge. You even know the terms. We're in business."

I put paper around the logs and Marge lit the match. We watched carefully for a few minutes to be sure the smoke was going upward and the fire was well controlled. The logs needed time to attain a steady burn, so we closed the grate and decided to pray while we waited.

I sat on the brick hearth, and Marge sat nearby on the floor while she offered up a prayer. "Lord, You see us right now, and You understand what we are trying to do. Mary is coming to You today to show You that she wants to live for You with all her heart, soul, and strength. She has renounced her past, and we thank You that You have forgiven her through Your precious blood that You shed at Calvary. We come today to cleanse this house as much as we are able and leave the rest to You. Thank You that You hear us. Thank You that You are here for us. If God be for us, who can be against us? Blessed be the name of the Lord."

We looked at the logs. Marge said, "I think the fire is ready. Let's get started."

Marge picked up a book and began to tear out the pages. I followed suit. I opened the grate, and we carefully tossed in hunks of pages. The fire leaped and licked hungrily as we fed it. We worked at a slow pace to keep the fire controlled.

Without realizing it, Marge and I had become subdued. We methodically tore pages and said intermittent, quiet prayers. Our fingers began to ache, but we kept tearing pages. "Mary, this is good. This is right."

"I know, Marge. I feel it too. These books contain abominable lies. I never want to be a perpetrator of that philosophy again. I don't want to give these books to anyone. I energetically propagated these lies. Now, I can do no less for Jesus. I must tell others what I have found. Actually, Marge, He found me. My heart still overflows when I think about it."

I tossed the last hunk of pages in the fire and closed the grate. Marge and I looked at each other. "Thanks, Marge. I'm so glad you were here."

"Me too, Mary. I've never experienced anything like this before. I can feel peace inside."

"Jesus is the Prince of Peace," I said. "I searched all of my adult life for peace. To me, it is a treasured gift."

It would be a while before the fire burned out. I looked at the small flames turning pages into ashes. "I've got an idea. Ruth mentioned anointing things with oil and praying. Let's go anoint Bob's books with oil and pray over them. We can't destroy his books, but we can ask the Lord to take care of them. Come on, Marge. I'll get the oil."

The only oil I had was a large bottle of vegetable oil for cooking. I took the tall bottle from the pantry shelf and met Marge in the bedroom.

I poured just a little oil on my fingers. Touching the bookcase I firmly stated, "I want these books out of this house in the name of the Lord Jesus Christ. As for me and my house, we will serve the Lord."

I looked at Marge. "I can't do it, but Jesus can. I'm confident of that wonderful name and the One it belongs to."

"He can handle it. Now I have to be going, Mary. It's time for kids and cooking and all of those daily type of things."

"I know, Marge. Thanks again for coming. I'll see you Sunday at church."

Chapter Eleven

The Impossible

"What are you doing, Bob?" The small commotion in the front bedroom pricked my curiosity and drew me to the doorway. Bob was in front of the bookcase and had a cardboard box on the floor beside him. Taking books from the shelves, he glanced at each one and then put it in the box.

"Oh, I'm just getting rid of some books," he said nonchalantly.

"You are? What books are you getting rid of?" I asked in careful tones.

"Mainly the ones I used to read when we were in that study group," he replied.

I leaned against the door frame and uttered a slight gasp of amazement. "H-how come you're doing that?"

"I don't know. I just thought I would clean out these shelves today," he answered noncommittally.

"Oh, okay," I said. Thinking that I had better leave well enough alone, I returned to the kitchen to mop the floor.

"Lord, You've done it again," I exclaimed in a whisper while I pushed the mop across the floor. "You really are the God of the impossible. I never said a word to Bob about his books. He didn't even give a reason for throwing them out. I'm impressed, God."

Bob carried his boxed-up books out to the trash and then came back in the house. Seeing him approach the kitchen floor, I hollered out, "Stop! Don't go in there. The floor is still drying."

"Oops! I almost did it," Bob said with one foot suspended over the threshold. Retracting his foot, he turned and joined me in the living room.

"Are we still going to that rock concert tonight?" I asked him.

"Sure," he said. "Why wouldn't we?"

"I was just checking," I answered.

Bob knew that I did not want to go to the concert. We had already been through the discussion about it. Everything in me recoiled at the thought of having to sit through a rock concert. Explaining my feelings to Bob had been futile. We were going and that was the end of the discussion.

While Bob showered, I took the opportunity to get on my knees in the bedroom. "Lord, You know my heart," I prayed. "You know that the concert is the last place I want to be. What I once loved, I now detest. You really are making me into a new creature in You, Lord, but I don't know how to handle this situation. What do I do now? Do I submit? Do I refuse? Help!"

I knelt there quietly for a minute or two. "Lord, I don't know what else to do but go. Please protect me. Please do something; I don't know what. Your Word says that husbands can be won without a word from us wives by beholding our chaste conversation, or manner of life. So I'm going to be quiet on this one, Lord, and let You deal with him again."

I got up from my knees and went to get myself ready to go. I stood in front of the mirror in tailored navy slacks and a pale yellow turtleneck under a plaid shirt with tiny lines in navy, red, and yellow. I had rolled my hair on large rollers in yet another ploy to tame the ever-present frizz. The smoothed, dark curls cascaded past my shoulders, and a tiny pearled stud glistened in each ear.

"Definitely a new creature," I mused to myself. Gone were the faded, hip-hugger jeans with torn knees. Gone were the baggy shirts and bare feet and thongs. More than that, gone were the days when I had no one to turn to for answers and help. "You will never leave me, Jesus. That's what Your Word says. You will teach me and lead me into all truth, whatever that means. I can depend on You." Attempting to lift my melancholy self up, I said more enthusiastically, "So! Let's go, Lord. We're off to a rock concert! Have You ever been to one of those, Lord?"

We arrived at the Summit in downtown Houston and circled the building to find the garage entrance. It's a good thing I didn't have to drive. Even though I grew up in the Houston vicinity, I have never fully conquered the mazes of freeways, exits, and signs. At sixty miles an hour, I usually miss the exit by the time I read the sign.

I told Bob how much I appreciated his driving capabilities as he turned into the parking garage. It was the most positive line of conversation I could think of at the moment. Somehow I knew that the only way to go through with this situation was with a right spirit. Since my case had already been stated, I figured that a calm and quiet attitude would speak much louder than grumbling.

Bob led me by the hand toward the ticket gates. We have always been hand holders. His huge hands totally enveloped and warmed mine. I clutched his a little tighter as we neared the sound vibrations emanating from inside the building. A small dart of fear passed through me. "That's funny," I thought. "I've never been scared of these things before. Lord, are You still there?" I mentally quizzed. "Whatever You do, Lord, don't leave me now. I need You more than ever. I don't want to go in there. Calm my insides, Lord."

We entered the darkness and groped our way up the aisle stairs. When we sat down, I took a deep breath in a sigh of small relief. That was a mistake. The air was permeated with the smell of marijuana. I quickly and easily recognized the familiar odor. "Oh, no," I muttered in a less than audible whisper.

As my eyes grew accustomed to the darkness, my senses received another assault. A young couple several rows in front of us were locked in a not-so-sweet embrace. I closed my eyes, but that only increased the pounding in my ears as the speakers propelled shocks through the air waves into every corner and crevice from ceiling to floor and wall to wall. It would have done no good to grumble at that point: Bob couldn't have heard me anyway.

The lights came on and intermission was announced. Whew! I thought. Half down and only half to go.

My thoughts of relief were premature, though. A gigantic screen was lowered, and another rock band was displayed on film. It was a band well-known for their satanic style. Their painted faces and wild gyrations glared in front of me. The sound theme from the movie *The Exorcist* was being played over the speakers.

"Oh, God! I can't bear any more of this. Please, please get me out of here," I silently prayed.

"I want a Coke, Bob. Let's go to the snack bar."

"Okay," he said, taking my hand in his.

As we waited in the snack-bar line, Bob said, "Sorry about that film, Mary. I didn't know they would put those guys on."

I gave a weak smile and nodded. I didn't dare open my mouth. I was doing good at keeping a quiet spirit, and I didn't want to ruin it. I knew inside that no matter what happened after tonight, I could never, ever go back to another rock concert. I would die first, I thought to myself for added emphasis.

We got popcorn and Cokes and made our way back into the darkened room. The snack helped divert my attention. I concentrated on the popcorn, savoring the flavor with the only sense I had left.

"Let's go," Bob suddenly said.

"Go? It's not quite over." Catching myself, I interjected, "Oh, okay, let's go." He had caught me by surprise, and I almost blew it.

I set the cups down and took hold of Bob's big hand again. He led me through the darkness into the front halls and out to the parking garage. I welcomed the chill of the night air with a deep breath. This time I was refreshed.

"I owe you one, Mary."

"What?" I asked looking at him in wonder.

"I didn't realize it would be like that."

"But, Bob, we've been to these things before. You knew what they are like."

"It seemed different tonight. I don't know why, but for some reason I just don't want to go back to these anymore," he said. "And besides that, I owe you one because you went with me. In fact, I think I owe you about ten."

I shivered in the chilly air, and Bob put his arm around me. I huddled close to him, but I couldn't quite stop shaking. The hand of God in my life was astounding me. God was undertaking the impossible for me. He was moving mountains.

One Sunday morning shortly after the concert incident, Bob and I were sitting in our usual pew. I would always sneak little glances at him, but Bob keeps a lot of his thoughts and feelings inside. When the sermon ended, I closed my eyes in prayer with everyone else. When I opened my eyes, Bob wasn't there.

Looking all around I thought, Where on earth did he go? It had not occurred to me that he could be walking down the aisle toward the front. Maybe he went to the men's room, I thought and then turned my attention to the front of the church.

Bob! That's Bob up there! He went forward to accept Jesus as his Savior! Wow! Fireworks were going off inside me. I wanted to leap for joy. I watched the proceedings with excitement. He was handed a card to fill out.

I can't believe it! What are they doing? What's with the card? My husband is getting saved and they hand him a card? Isn't anybody excited about this besides me? I calmed down a bit. "Well, Lord, I'm excited. And You're probably excited. The angels are probably excited. I haven't been around here long enough to see anybody get saved, so I guess this is the way it's done."

I went to the front to join Bob. He gave me a big

smile. "I've been thinking about this for a while," he said.

The pastor came over and shook Bob's hand. They chatted for a few minutes, and people we had been getting to know gathered around us. After a short visit with our friends, Bob and I were ready to track down our four children.

As we were leaving, Marge came to me and gave me a big hug. "How can two walk together except they be agreed? Now you can live for God as a family, Mary."

"I know, Marge. We've been praying for a year for this. I'm excited."

Putting a large book in my hands, Marge said, "Here's something for you to read. It might have more answers for you."

I looked at the cover. It was entitled *Kingdom of the Cults* by Walter Martin. "Thanks, Marge. I'll look at it this afternoon."

Bob had gone to get the children and was back to get me. "Let's go, Mary. We've got hungry kids."

"See you later, Marge," I said as Bob was whisking me away by the arm.

After lunch I waited until the children were occupied before I picked up the book that Marge had given to me. Dwayne, Keven, and Jennifer were sprawled in various corners of the bunk beds reading Garfield comics. Jeffery went from one sibling to the other as they took turns reading to him.

Curling up in the couch corner, I began to scan through the large book. Bob had commented in the past about my idiosyncrasy of starting in the middle of books instead of at the beginning. I was also notorious for reading five or six books concurrently. For some reason, my sense of wanting things in order did not apply to books. The end result was that I read them from cover to cover, and the process was accomplished according to the priority of my interests.

Scanning through the large book, I assessed the layout, purpose, and goal of the author. I was immediately intrigued by the purpose of the book. The author had taken a list of doctrinal groups, and using their own material, Mr. Martin compared them with the Scriptures. The layout was well done, making the comparisons obvious. The index listed the various doctrines addressed. I was hooked. I turned to chapter one and began reading.

Chapter one was very short. The children were still well occupied in the back bedroom, so I happily began chapter two. Reading with interest, I came quickly to the second page of that chapter when I stopped and sat up straight. A phrase had caught my eye: "the subtle art of redefinition."

It was as if a light was flashing the word *priority* in my brain. With intense focus, I began to speed-read the next couple of pages until I came to this paragraph:

> The Christian must realize that for every biblical or doctrinal term he mentions, a redefinition light flashes on in the mind of the cultist, and a lightning-fast redefinition is accomplished. Realizing that the cultist will apparently agree with the doctrine under discussion, while firmly disagreeing in reality with the historical and Biblical concept, the Christian is on his way to dealing effectively with cult terminology.

This was the puzzle piece I had been looking for. Many

people sitting in Christian churches on Sunday mornings can be found sitting in study groups like the one Bob and I were in on Tuesday nights. Occult philosophy (New Age) deceivingly weaves half truths within it and often uses a Scripture quotation to reinforce the deception.

Quoting Scripture can give the appearance of truth while in reality the person is speaking a lie. By taking verses out of context and redefining the content, a person can seemingly agree with a Christian and yet have a completely different concept. That is why I was able to converse with Mardel for hours before the conflict surfaced. I had known enough pieces of Scripture to make spiritual conversation even with my untrained mind. Through my years in the occult, no one ever crossed me or confronted me with real truth until I met Mardel. She had been reading the Bible for years, and her senses were trained. When I talked about reincarnation, Mardel quickly refuted it.

The devil's strategy has been the same since the beginning of time. In Genesis chapter three, Satan quoted God's words to Eve in the first verse, but he put the words into question form, causing doubt to enter Eve's mind: "Yea, hath God said, Ye shall not eat of every tree of the garden?"

Then, in verse four, the devil blatantly contradicted God's words: "Ye shall not surely die." When doubt entered Eve's mind, she gave place to the devil, and he was able to deceive her. The interesting thing was that the devil used God's Word in the deception.

The Gospel according to John describes the devil as a murderer and a liar. The most dangerous form of a lie is a lie with a half truth mixed in it. A mind that is not trained to discern between good and evil accepts the half truth and ingests the half lie with it. The writer of Hebrews provides the antidote for deception: "But strong meat belongeth to them that are of full age, even those who by reason of use have their senses exercised to discern both good and evil" (Hebrews 5:14).

The spiritually mature person is one who has been consistently using, or reading, the Word of God until his senses are exercised unto discernment. Church attendance alone is not enough spiritual food to maintain a spiritual life. The devil is subtle, and he knows Scripture. When the devil tempted Jesus, he used Scripture, but Jesus countered with more Scripture. After three unsuccessful attempts, the devil left. Jesus is the Word made flesh, and He used the written Word to combat the devil. How much more do we need to hide the Word of God in our hearts that we might not sin against Him?

My program of daily Bible reading destroyed the boulder of lies in my mind, but the fragmented pieces that were left caused confusion. Mr. Martin's explanation about redefining words and Scripture cleared away the confusion. I put the book down and ran to the bedroom to get on my knees.

"Lord, You have answered the second half of my prayer. Through Ruth You answered the first half by explaining the devil's network, or hierarchy, and his ability to transform himself into an angel of light. Now, through this book, I can see how I was able to think of myself as Christian while I was in the depth of deception. I can see how I was able to talk to Christians through the years and seem to be in agreement with them. The Christians were fooled too. I used to talk freely about You,

Jesus, but my definition was of another Jesus. Your Word destroyed the deception and has been retraining my senses. Now I can feel the pieces coming together. Please take the fragmented lies and cleanse them away, Lord," I prayed fervently.

As I arose from that prayer, I knew that I would never again be able to effortlessly expound the occult philosophy. My mind was cleansed. The fragments were gone, replaced with a deeper peace than I had known before.

This proved true later when I became a witness to others caught in deception. When I was questioned about my previous beliefs, the Word of God surfaced instead of the occult philosophy. Using Scripture, I would explain the devil's wiles instead of the intricacies of the occult. This was a delight to me because it did more good for the questioner than the details they were originally looking for.

As I left the bedroom, I paused to look at a card I had taped on the door. It was made of heavy, lavender paper and had a message typed on it in bold print. Ruth had given it to me. I had put it on the door in order to read it every day when I woke up in the morning and when I went to bed at night. It read: "With Men This Is Impossible, But With God All Things Are Possible, Matthew 19:26."

"How many times have I looked at this card, Lord? Now, Bob's books are gone. I don't have to go to any more rock concerts. Bob has accepted You as his Savior. My mind is cleansed. With You, Jesus, all things are possible."

Chapter Twelve

The Doctors

The large carpeted inset in the middle of the mall provided a great place for small children to run and jump and tumble. I sat on the surrounding marble ledge and watched Jeffery expend his energy. My weekdays at home were isolated from adult companionship since most of the women in the neighborhood held outside jobs. Occasionally, I would take Jeffery to the mall so that I could be around people for a while.

Jeff was having a great time, and I enjoyed watching him play. I also watched people as they walked by. Perhaps some people watchers observe sizes, shapes, mannerisms, and clothing; I was mesmerized by movement. I watched people walking with brisk steps. Their faces were preoccupied with shopping or talking to their companions. I noticed that they were able to do these things effortlessly, and I felt jealous.

My range of movement consisted of driving to the mall and sitting while Jeff ran and jumped. The marble ledges confined my young son so that I would not have to run after him. As much as I enjoyed watching Jeffery, I was jealous that I did not have the energy that I perceived in other people. Two young mothers were passing by me. One was pushing a stroller and the other was carrying her toddler. They were laughing and talking while they moved freely through the mall. Obviously, they were unaware of the energy required by their bodies to walk, talk, and carry children.

I rubbed my lower back with one hand and supported myself with the other hand. It was all I could do to sit up much less walk around the mall. Carrying Jeff was out of the question. Why? I wondered. Why can't I be like other people? Why are most of my days spent just trying to function? Could it have been the hepatitis? It seems like this terrible weakness began after that. Is this back pain a residual effect from the car accident I had at age eighteen? But other people have had accidents or hepatitis. They weren't in this shape years later, were they? And why am I getting worse instead of better? I eat a balanced diet and take vitamins. The chiropractors keep my curved spine in alignment weekly. I walk every day for exercise. After all that, I still can hardly move. These same thoughts and questions circled in my mind frequently. My family doctor labeled me healthy, which added confusion to my pain and malaise.

"Come on, Jeffy. Let's go home," I called to my active three-year-old.

Jeffery went dashing past me. I got up and went down the two steps to wait for Jeff's next lap. I was ready to catch him by the hand and announce more firmly that we were in fact leaving.

As soon as I got home, I put a Snoopy video on for Jeffery and went to lie down. Relief washed over me. Lying still enabled me to catch my breath. After thirty minutes of rest, my mind and spirit were ready to get up, but my body rebelled. Just a few more minutes, I thought.

Five minutes passed far too quickly, and then another three minutes ticked away. I must get up. There is too much to do to lie here any longer, I firmly ordered myself. I felt drugged, as if I had to struggle to overcome gravity to get up from the bed or even lift my arms.

Determination won the day, and I got up. By sheer strength of will, I made it through the afternoon chores and evening cooking routine. After dinner, Bob handed me a card. It had the name and phone number of a doctor of internal medicine on it. "I was talking to some people at work about you, Mary. Someone gave me this doctor's name. I want you to make an appointment and go see him."

Specialists have full schedules, and this doctor was no exception. I waited three weeks for the appointment. Dr. L's nurse wrote down my medical history and then took my blood pressure. "Eighty over fifty," she stated unconcernedly.

"It's always that low," I said. "Is that why I feel so tired?"

"No, probably not," she answered. "Some people just have low blood pressure." Then she left the room.

The nurse came in with the doctor as he began his examination. "We are going to take a lot of tests, Mary. The nurse will draw blood today for a complete workup, and I want you to come in Friday for a six-hour glucose tolerance test. If there is anything wrong, we will find it," Dr. L said in a cold, professional tone.

In spite of the doctor's unfriendly manner, I felt encouraged by the battery of tests. He's a specialist, I thought to myself. He can find the problem and I will be all fixed up. I'll be able to function like everybody else.

The test instructions ordered fasting, so I arrived at the doctor's office Friday morning hungry but hopeful. The nurse gave me a huge cup of sickeningly sweet fluid to drink. She drew blood, and then I gulped down the fluid. "Now go sit in the waiting room, and I will draw your blood again in an hour," instructed the nurse.

I searched through the stacks of sports and fishing magazines looking for a ladies magazine to occupy the passing time. Finding some reading material more suited to my feminine interests, I settled down to read about child rearing, home decor, and tried and true recipes. Between articles, I watched other patients come and go. When the hour was up, the nurse drew blood again, and I resumed my post in the waiting room.

Hunger was my only discomfort for four hours. The nurse drew blood and sent me back to the waiting room. I had read the two ladies magazines from cover to cover and wondered how to further occupy the remaining hours. I didn't have to wonder too long because a tremor began to shake me as I sat in the chair. Uh oh. I feel funny. I had better find something to read to take my mind off it, I thought.

Before I could begin a search for another magazine, I broke out into a sweat. The tremor progressed to a noticeable and uncontrollable shaking. I went through the door to find the nurse. "Ma'am? Nurse? Somebody?"

I leaned against the wall. The nurse came around the corner. "You don't look so good."

"It's getting dark. I can't see," I stated weakly.

"You're fainting. Come lie on this stretcher," she ordered.

"Stretcher? Where's a stretcher? I can't see."

When I opened my eyes, I was lying on a stretcher. The nurse handed me a Coke to drink. "Here, drink this. It will raise your blood sugar, and you will feel better. There's a vending machine in the hall. You can get some peanut-butter crackers to help also. Then the doctor will see you in his office for a consultation."

A few sips of Coke revived me, and I sat up. When the fog in my head began to clear, I bought some crackers and nibbled on them until I felt stable enough to walk. The nurse took me into one of the examination rooms to talk to the doctor.

"Well, Mary, it looks like you are a bit hypoglycemic, just borderline though. It's nothing to worry about. Eat six small meals throughout the day instead of three large meals. Small, frequent meals will help keep your blood sugar constant. You're a little on the anemic side also. Here is a prescription for some vitamins with iron. Other than that, you're in good shape."

"I am? Oh, good. I will gladly take iron and eat little meals to feel better. That's simple," I said as I envisioned wonderful improvement through these minor changes.

I felt happy that night as I related the doctor's words to Bob. "It's just blood sugar and iron, Bob; that's all I need to watch and I will feel better."

"I'm glad you went to him, Mary. I know he checked you out thoroughly. Be sure to do exactly as he instructed."

"Are you kidding? I'll do anything to feel normal. I'm desperate."

I began taking the vitamins right away and started a schedule of six small meals each day. There were good days and bad days. I tried to ignore the bad days and told myself I needed more time for my body to make adjustments.

Obviously, this is a bad day, I thought when I woke up one morning and didn't have the strength to get out of bed. I called Dr. L's office and made another appointment.

"Ninety over sixty," said the nurse as she removed the blood pressure cuff from my arm.

"Are you sure that doesn't make me tired?" I asked the nurse again.

"No, some people just have low blood pressure," she restated.

Dr. L came in and made a brief examination. "Are you eating six small meals per day and taking iron?"

"Yes," I assured him.

"You're fine. You're healthy," said Dr. L.

"Why do I feel so bad?" I asked him.

"I don't know why. I think it's in your mind," said Dr. L.

"My mind! Do you think I'm making this up?" I asked, fearing his answer.

"No. I think you really feel bad, but I think the problem is in your mind. I can't help you, Mary. Go see a psychiatrist."

Dr. L turned and left the room. I sat there dumbfounded. All of the encouragement and hope I had felt weeks ago left me. I picked up my purse and left the room with my head down. I didn't want to see the other patients as I walked through the waiting room to leave. When I got in the car, I leaned my head on the steering wheel and cried until I felt empty. I drove home with my senses numbed.

That evening I told Bob about my conversation with the doctor. Then I said, "I don't think it's in my mind, Bob. My back hurts; my blood pressure is low. How can I be making this up?"

"He didn't say you were making it up, Mary."

"That's what he meant, isn't it?" I looked at Bob for even a glint of hope and understanding.

"We'll just wait and see. Keep taking your iron and eating frequent, small meals. Maybe you'll feel better in time."

At least Bob wasn't treating me like a mental case. I took courage in his words. "That's it. I probably just need more time."

Time proved us both wrong though. As I dragged through the days, I truly was becoming depressed. I read in a book that energy begets energy. The author wrote that inactivity will cause depression and rob a person of energy. The advice was to get up and go. It's worth a try, I thought.

I made myself get up. I made myself move and work and walk. Instead of getting stronger and better, I would fall on the bed in weakness and in tears. The physical weakness and pain was intensified with the torment of Dr. L's diagnosis. His words rang in my ears: "It's in your mind."

Dwayne and Keven's mother was studying to be a chiropractor and had contacts through the college. She gave me the name of an osteopath who treated his patients through vitamin and herb therapy. I was ready to try anything and called for an appointment.

Dr. W's nurse was taking my blood pressure. "Eighty over fifty!" she exclaimed. "How are you even walking around?"

I looked at the nurse. "Do you mean that my low blood pressure contributes to this awful feeling I have?"

"Why, of course it does," she affirmed.

"Another nurse told me that it wasn't a problem."

"Well, I'm surprised you're walking around," the nurse said.

Dr. W came into the room. He was a warm, friendly man. He shook my hand and began to ask me questions to get a medical history. "I will do a lot of testing and get back with you."

"I had another doctor tell me the same thing, Dr. W."

"We do things a little differently here, Mary. Just give me some time, and let's see what we can find."

The nurse and lab technician came in with bottles and vials. The nurse drew blood and then picked up scissors. "What are you going to do?" I asked her.

"I'm going to cut a small piece of hair from the nape of your neck. We will send it off for a hair analysis," she answered.

I was skeptical. "That's different, all right."

The nurse smiled. "We do this all the time. Actually, it's a very informative test. It gives us levels of minerals and nutrients in your system, or the lack thereof."

When the testing was completed, I made an appointment to come back for the results. After supper, I filled Bob in on the friendly doctor's office with the strange tests. As usual, Bob's approach was, "Let's wait and see." Bob's predictability soothed my frazzled nerves and helped me to take that "wait and see" attitude with him.

The morning of test results arrived. Bob had already left for work when I heard Jennifer's voice calling me. "Mom! Look outside! It's snowing."

"Snowing!" I remarked with unbelief. I had grown up in the Houston area and had seen snow very few times in my life. When it did snow, however, it was always in February, and this was February.

I looked out through my bedroom window. What could have been rain was, upon closer inspection, actually snow. The tiny flakes were not much bigger than raindrops, but they floated softly down, unlike pelting rain. The flakes melted on contact with the warm ground, since Houston's short winters rarely lower the ground temperature enough to hold snow.

"Do I have to go to school today?" Jennifer asked with anticipation.

"Yes, Jennifer. I'm sure the bus will be here. There's not enough snow to play in anyway. It just looks pretty falling from the sky and decorating the housetops." Jennifer and I stood gazing out of the window. We were drinking in the uncommon sight. The white overlay glistened on the rooftops and on the bare branches of trees. Icicles gleamed from the eaves on the neighbor's house.

It was hard to turn away from the quiet and beautiful scene. "Go get dressed, Jennifer. I will fix your lunch bag. The bus will be here soon."

Jennifer's bus was on time, so I didn't think there would be a road problem later in the day. When time came for my doctor's appointment, I bundled up Jeffery and we got in the car. The car radio announced ice hazards on the roads. Oh no, I thought. I've waited for today to get my test results. I hope I don't run into any ice.

I drove the mile around the subdivision to the main highway. When I pulled out onto the highway, the back end of the car slid across the road toward the shoulder. Unaccustomed to icy streets, I panicked. The ice was patchy, however, and I was able to stop the car on drier ground. Knowing my Southern driving skills were no match for this weather, I carefully turned the car around and went back home. Test results would have to wait for another day. I wanted to be alive to get them.

My rescheduled appointment was for the following week. Weather can change daily in this locality, and my next trip to the doctor's office only required a light sweater. The nurse took me into an examination room and charted the required vital signs.

Dr. W came into the room and greeted me. "You look well. How do you feel?"

"Hi, Dr. W," I said ignoring the "How do you feel" question.

"There is good color in your face and you have a nice smile. One would never know it to look at you, Mary, but my tests show that your system is surprisingly down."

I looked straight at him. Thank God, I thought. Someone is taking me seriously.

"I'm going to put you on potent vitamin therapy. I'm sure we can have you feeling better in a couple of months."

I left the doctor's office with an armload of bottles filled with vitamins and herbs. Hope had surfaced again.

Every morning and evening I took the prescribed

pills, capsules, and potions. I stayed away from junk food and filled in a regular diet of meat, vegetables, fruits, and grains with sprouts, seeds, and juices. Periodically I reported to Dr. W's office for a checkup.

"Your blood pressure is still eighty over fifty," said the nurse. "Are you feeling any better?"

Normally I tried to hide behind a healthy-looking countenance even to the doctors. Abhorring the thought of ever being labeled a hypochondriac, I had trained myself to put on a happy face. But on this day, I was slumped in a chair. "No," I responded. "If anything, I feel worse. I can't sit up. Please help me."

Dr. W came into the room. "What's wrong, Mary? You don't look too great today."

"I don't know. I just can hardly sit up."

He studied me for a minute. "I'm going to put you in the hospital. I need to test you for things that I don't have equipment for here in the office. I think the bed rest will do you good too. You are in a state of exhaustion."

Ziklag

Greetings from the ashes of Ziklag,
Birthplace of victories unseen.
Cheers amidst tears at Ziklag,
The future belongs to the King!

There's smoke all around here at Ziklag;
Restoration looks hopeless and vain;
But the end is not yet here at Ziklag;
The Lord of hosts, the King of glory, doth reign!

O heart, find a place here at Ziklag
To see how His glory doth shine.
Keep fixed on His glory at Ziklag;
From these ruins you will see the divine!

Be patient, gather courage at Ziklag;
Your King will soon shout, "Pursue!"
You will rise from the ruins at Ziklag,
If to Him only you will remain but true.

Phyllis Buckner

Chapter Thirteen

Beauty and the Beast

The nurse came into the room with a wheelchair. "Hi, Mrs. Ellis. I've come to take you down for an ultrasound."

I climbed out of bed and put on my bright yellow robe, tying it at the waist. "I'm ready," I said as I sat in the wheelchair.

"You're certainly cooperative," said the nurse. "I can tell when someone really wants to get well, because they will do whatever is necessary."

"That's where I am," I told her. "I will do anything I can to feel like a regular person again."

The table was cold and hard, but I lay still as the technician rubbed some oily liquid under my rib cage. She moved the disc-shaped instrument back and forth over the oil. "Why are you making those faces?" she asked me.

"It hurts," I answered. "Making faces is quieter than fussing, so I'm just making faces."

"Ultrasounds don't hurt," the technician abruptly informed me.

"This one does," I replied.

There was another technician in the room also, and the two of them looked at each other. I got the distinct impression that they did not believe me. I closed my eyes and tried to relax, hoping to lessen the pain. These girls have seen many ultrasounds. I'm sure they know what they are talking about. If it's not supposed to hurt, why does it? I asked myself. I don't dare ask them; they obviously don't even believe me.

"We're through. You can get up now," said the one holding the instrument.

I climbed down from the table and began to walk forward. The pain was so intense where she had been pressing that I leaned against a wall trying to catch my breath. Wanting to get out of the room, I was trying to get enough composure to walk. I took one step and then slumped forward, clutching my ribs and bursting into tears.

The nearby technician caught me, and the two of them assisted me back on the table. I felt a cold, wet cloth over my face and heard a much gentler voice say, "Mrs. Ellis, be sure and tell your doctor about this. It's not normal for an ultrasound to hurt this way."

Someone came with a wheelchair, and I was taken back to my room. Exhaustion well describes it, I thought to myself, remembering the doctor's words. I just want to lie down and not move.

The phone next to the bed began to ring soon after I was back in the bed. I looked at it and counted the rings. I didn't have the strength left to reach for it. When the ringing stopped, I listened to the silence. It felt as if an insurmountable brick wall were surrounding me. It was a wall of pain beyond which I could no longer reach out to other people; my own need was too great.

"Lord," I prayed silently, "Your understanding is unsearchable. You never grow weary or faint. I don't understand what is happening to me or why I can't overcome this wall that seems to surround me. Please help me. Please let me find out what's wrong and get it fixed. I can't go on like this anymore."

My Bible was in the drawer of the bedside table. Many times during those five days in the hospital I would take it out and hold it. Sometimes I would read one verse and then lie still and think about it. My mind was unable to take in whole chapters. A particular verse of Scripture became a lifeline for me: "They that wait upon the LORD shall renew their strength; they shall mount up with wings as eagles; they shall run, and not be weary; and they shall walk, and not faint" (Isaiah 40:31).

My sister Phyllis came to visit me and brought a small gift. It was a rock she had painted. A little cross was painted on one side, and a slip of paper was glued to the other side. When I opened the piece of paper, I found Isaiah 40:31 typed on it. "Oh, Phyllis, I love it," I said, reaching up to hug her.

That rock stayed on the bedside table. I quoted the verse from Isaiah over and over and over. It became my own special promise from the Lord.

Another thing I filled my mind with during the wall of pain captivity was a song I knew from being in the church choir. It was from a Christmas cantata. The words went like this:

Wonderful name, Jesus.
Wonderful name, Jesus.
Name angels sang, the night all heaven rang,
Wonderful name, Jesus.

Mary was the first to hear it,
Name that came from heaven above.
Name that raises souls from darkness,
This the only name worth singing of.

This song would float through my mind, bringing comfort and peace when the pain and questions tried to force their way in. I would go to sleep singing the chorus and wake up to sing it again. When I couldn't concentrate enough to read and didn't have the strength to carry on conversations, I would lie still and let the words float through my mind again: "Wonderful name, Jesus."

About midweek, I was resting quietly when a cheery voice interrupted my mental songfest. My older sister, Carol, came bubbling into the room. Being sanguine from the tip of her pert little nose to the soles of her feet, Carol had me laughing within minutes. Her own life was anything but rosy, and yet her stream of effervescent bubbles never seemed to dissipate. By the time Carol rose to leave, I was holding my sides from laughter. I waved goodbye as she called out, "Toodles!" I could hear her quick steps as she bounced more than walked down the hall.

Now that's a ball of energy, I thought as a smile lingered on my face.

On Friday, Dr. W came into the room. Bob was there with me. The doctor looked at both of us and said, "I've run every test I can think of. Everything comes back normal."

The brick wall I had pictured in my mind seemed closer and higher. I had thought I was at the bottom of the pit, but the pit was yawning deeper now. Hope was winging its way out the window. I was in pain for no reason. All reasons and excuses were stripped from me. With a diagnosis of health, I was thrown back into the world of expectations. I would be expected to get up and function. "I will," I declared with defiance at my body and determination in my mind.

When I arrived back home, I threw myself into the duties of daily life. It only lasted a few days, though. One morning I woke up and didn't move. There was nothing left, no strength, no energy. No amount of willpower could change it.

Jennifer made herself ready for school and caught the bus. Jeff woke up and joined me on the bed. I turned on Sesame Street for him, and we watched it together.

"I'm hungry, Mommy."

"I know, Jeff. Watch Mr. Rogers now."

When Mr. Rogers was over, the inevitable request came again: "I'm hungry, Mommy."

I had to get up. There was no choice. Jeff was too small to take care of himself. I pushed myself up from the bed. The familiar feeling of having to overcome gravity for every movement overwhelmed me. Slowly, I walked to the kitchen. I made Jeff a quick breakfast and filled his plastic cup. I set the food and drink within his reach and went back to bed.

When Jeff finished eating, he joined me on the bed again. "Jeff, bring your blocks, books, and toys in here. You can play right beside me, okay?"

The next day was the same, and so was the next. My world shriveled to the bed, the most necessary of activities, and church on Sundays. Somehow I always made it to church, which was the highlight of my week. Every worship service still held wonder and beauty for me.

Church provided contact with my friends, relieving the isolation I experienced throughout the week. Teaching a Sunday school class of seventh-grade girls was the one vehicle of outward expression remaining in my life. Preparing for the class was a bright spot in my dreadful weeks. Instead of draining me, teaching Sunday school energized me. I loved it. The Word of God changed my life, and sharing it with others was exhilarating in my spirit no matter what shape my body was in.

To those outside my immediate family and very closest of friends, I appeared well and fine. Only my family and my prayer partners, Judy and Marge, saw me during the week. One day, Judy and Marge came over to clean my house for me. Their kindness should be uppermost in my memory, but a lesson stands out from that experience: the lesson of receiving. My pride died a thousand deaths when those ladies cleaned house for me. I would have given anything to be cleaning for them and doing things for others.

Pride didn't go down easily. As I lay on the couch and watched Judy and Marge vacuum and dust, a buried emotion surfaced. It was anger. At first I didn't realize that I was fuming. The longer I lay there, the angrier I became. Where is this coming from? I wondered. What am I mad about and at whom?

Hiding my feelings from Marge and Judy, I visited with them before they left. They each gave me a big hug, and I thanked them profusely. When they were gone I went back to bed and stared at the ceiling. What am I so mad about? Who am I mad at? Whatever and whoever it is, I'm boiling mad. Here I am stuck in this bed, and everyone else is up and about. I'm hurting and there's no reason for it.

A feeling of desperation swept over me. I can't even clean my own house. I'm of no use to anyone. I'm worthless and useless. I wish I could die. Why don't You let me die, God? Why couldn't You at least let me have a name for this enemy. What am I? Who am I? Isn't what we do tied up with who we are? Since I can't do anything, I'm a nobody, a nothing. This isn't living, it's existing. O God, somehow help me make it through today. How about helping me make it through the next five minutes?

A measure of calmness returned to my tumultuous thoughts. "That's it!" I said with my eyes closed. "Five minutes, Lord; I need You for five minutes. Then I need You the next five minutes. Let's get through this five minutes at a time. O God, I've never felt such despair."

I got up and went to the kitchen. Taking a brown paper bag, I opened the cabinet door and stretched my arm behind the bottles of vitamins and herbs. I began pushing bottles into the bag. I pitched, tossed, and pushed bottles into the bag until the cabinet was empty. "No more!" I stated flatly. "I'm through with these. I am not feeling one bit better. These are not the answer."

Dropping into a kitchen chair I mumbled, "I don't know what the answer is."

When Bob came home, I told him that I had thrown away all of the pills and potions. I was afraid he would be upset because of the expense of what I had thrown away, but desperation outweighed fear. To my surprise, Bob was in agreement with me about tossing the pills. "They haven't helped you," he said. "We need to look another direction."

Weeks of pain, exhaustion, and despair passed by. Bob came home from work with another doctor's name. This one was also a doctor of internal medicine. Being virtually bedridden, I had nothing to lose. I went to see him.

Dr. S took my case history as the others had done before him. Then he began to question me about stress. Bob was with me for this appointment, and he spoke up before I did. "She's had a lot of stress," he answered. "She was under stress for several years before I married her. When we married, we each had children. Step families are not easy and Mary is still under stress."

"I think that's your problem, Mary," said Dr. S. "Your body has become depleted of certain hormones needed to withstand stress. I know that you are wanting to get up, but I'm going to give you medicine that will actually put you back down. This other doctor you've told me about was right. You are in a state of exhaustion. I'm going to treat it in another manner, though. By putting you on antidepressants, we will allow your system to get the rest it needs. You will feel knocked out for a while, but if you will bear with me I think we can have you up and running again."

"I'm willing to try," I said.

The medicine caused horrible nightmares in vivid color. I slept all night and into the next day. Submerged into unconsciousness, I was unaroused by sounds or the activity of my family around me. When I regained consciousness, I called the doctor. "I can't take this," I reported. "I've been unconscious since yesterday. I have a small child. I cannot risk the inability to hear him and respond to him."

"Take half of a tablet, Mary."

"I'll try it on the weekend when Bob is here," I told him.

I could not tolerate half of a tablet. The doctor changed prescriptions several times over a period of weeks. They were all too strong. "Psychiatrists specialize in these types of medications," Dr. S said. "I want you to go to this man."

I looked at the card and then at Dr. S.

"You don't have to go through his therapy, Mary. I think he will know of a medication that you can tolerate; that's all. Will you go?"

I went. The psychiatrist brought me into his office and began to question me. Then he began to give me his suggestions. "Relax," he said. "Meditate."

He began to describe meditation and relaxation techniques. He didn't get too far, because I quickly recognized what he was talking about. "I know exactly what you are saying, doctor, and I won't do it. I used to meditate like that, but not anymore."

I started to tell the psychiatrist all about Jesus and how the Lord changed my life for the better. Even in the hard place that I was in, I still had the peace of knowing that the Lord was with me. The psychiatrist wrote a prescription and ushered me out of his office. "This is the weakest type of medication in the antidepressant family," he said. "Take only half a tablet at a time."

I was glad to be out of there, and he was glad to get me out. I tried the medication and was able to tolerate it. Reporting back to Dr. S, I stayed on the medication for a while. Using a daily journal, I kept track of everything I ate and made short entries about events and circumstances. I was hoping to find clues to my dilemma and help solve the problem.

Included in the journal were notes about daily Bible reading and talks to the Lord. Years later I looked back at the journal and understood how the Lord used that dark time in my life to draw me ever so near to Him and teach me things that I would have never learned any other way.

Phyllis brought me a little paper about my name. It said that the name Mary is associated with a bitter herb that when crushed gives forth a sweet fragrance. I added this paper to my treasures from Phyllis. Phyllis and Carol had both come to know Jesus, and I felt that the Lord was using them to encourage me. I clung to the definition of Mary. It gave me hope that good would come out of the pain.

The weeks turned into months, and no improvement was in sight. I looked at the antidepressant in my hand. This isn't the answer either, I thought, and I threw it in the garbage.

Lying on the bed, I was staring at the ceiling again. "What is this nameless physical enemy? How can I fight a foe with no substance. Give me a reason for the pain and exhaustion, or I am doomed to the disgrace of hypochondria. I've tried everything, Lord. How can You do this to me? I have figured it out. You're the one I'm mad at, Lord." I closed my eyes and waited.

"But you have not sweat blood."

My eyes opened instantly. "You're right, Lord. I haven't sweat blood. You *do* know, don't You? You really can be touched with our infirmities, can't You? You left heaven's glory and felt the pain of this world. You didn't have to do it, Lord. Oh, forgive me."

A verse of Scripture came to my mind: "I am crucified with Christ: nevertheless I live; yet not I, but Christ liveth in me: and the life which I now live in the flesh I live by the faith of the Son of God, who loved me, and gave himself for me" (Galatians 2:20).

The Lord was talking to me by bringing His written Word to my mind. The words I had read before now had substance and meaning. My understanding was opened, and I realized what the Lord was saying to me. The message was this: "You want to die, but I want you to live. The death you have been wishing for can come when you die to your own desires and live unto Me."

Tears rolled down my cheeks. "I understand, Lord! I see what You want. You have been working on me a long time to bring me to this place. I have been rebelling against You as I lay in this bed. I won't kick against the pricks anymore, Lord. Have Your way in my life. You loved me while I was yet a sinner. You bought me with a price, the price of Your own blood. If bed is what You have for me, then that's where I will stay. I'm going to rest in You, Lord. I'm tired."

Relaxation flowed through my body. The tense muscles let go. I quit worrying about my reputation. "If everyone thinks I'm a hypochondriac, let them. I'm living to please You, Lord. If nobody understands the pain, so what? You do, Lord. If I'm tensed and stressed, so what? You're the wonderful Counselor, Lord. And I can't be a nobody, because You died for me, Lord. That makes me somebody. I will quit finding places to hide. You are my hiding place, Lord. You are my refuge."

Peace, wonderful peace calmed my body and soul. I rested to my heart's content. False guilt was vanquished and healing had begun. New thoughts brimmed in my mind: The Lord wants me alive. He has work for me to do. He's not finished with me yet.

A desire and an excitement to live rose up in me. My inward thoughts turned outward in thanksgiving and praise to the Lord. My life was in His hands, and I knew it. He had already become my anchor and my rock. Now He was becoming my hope.

"There's one more thing I'd like to talk to You about, Lord. It's Carol. I've always wanted to be like Carol. She's so much fun. Everybody loves her to pieces. I love her too. Why can't I be like Carol?"

The wonderful Counselor has an answer for everything. This was His answer to me:

She's full of laughter;
You are full of tears.
She brings fun and sunshine;
You bring compassion and understanding.
  So different,
    Each unique,
      Both fashioned by God.

I started crying, which made me laugh. "You're right, God. I am full of tears. I'm beginning to understand that You made me the way that I am. Keep working with me, Lord. I love You."

The Beast

Apprehended, enslaved, forced to submit;
Against such power I had no wit.
Frightened and alone and compelled to serve;
Imprisoned I was, shaken, unnerved.

My love He would be waiting for
In His dark and hidden domain;
My captor was relentless,
and I sensed it caused Him pain.

It was the old fabled story of the beauty and the
beast;
I struggled against His terrible love,
yet knew it would not cease.

I saw my familiar world fade, as His world
became my home,
and day by day I found Him gentle,
and ceased my heart to roam.

I began to desire His presence, and seek His
awesome face,
I learned to call Him Lord and understand His
majestic grace.
But the greatness of His love, I was slow to
comprehend,
until at last my great facade His loving hands
did rend.

And truth revealed not my great heart,
for it had loved the least,
but, oh, the love of the Beauty's heart,
for I had been the beast.

Phyllis Buckner

Chapter Fourteen

Helen

"What one thing stands out in your mind that you have learned in Sunday school this year?" I asked of the seventh- and eighth-grade girls.

One young lady raised her hand without hesitation. "I know what it is for me," she declared. "It is the importance of reading my Bible. I never used to read it before, but since you have been our teacher, Mrs. Ellis, I have been reading the Bible every day."

When the young lady finished speaking, another girl raised her hand. "Me too," she said before I called her name.

A lump came up in my throat. I had expected to get all sorts of answers, but this one was above and beyond my expectations. If these girls learned nothing else but to read the Bible for themselves, then they would have learned the most valuable lesson I could have taught them. I once read that it is better to teach a person to plant than to give him bread. One slice of bread will temporarily stave off the hunger, but learning to plant ensures future meals.

I knew that Bible reading alone was not enough. The Scriptures admonish us in Hebrews chapter ten not to forsake the assembling of ourselves together. Likewise, the Epistle of Romans clearly teaches the necessity of hearing the preached Word of God: "How then shall they call on him in whom they have not believed? and how shall they believe in him of whom they have not heard? and how shall they hear without a preacher?" (Romans 10:14). These girls faithfully attended church services, but now they were adding the dimension of feeding on God's Word to nourish them in their spiritual growth.

The other girls didn't even raise their hands. They all began to speak at once. "I'm reading my Bible too," stated the next one. "Mrs. Ellis, I wish you would teach us this coming year too," said one. "We are going to miss you as our teacher," said another.

I looked at each one of them. "I will miss you all too. It has been a joy to share God's Word with you."

The strong impression to withdraw from teaching Sunday school puzzled me. My health and strength were improving slowly. I had no apparent reason to cease a responsibility that was more of a joy to me than a burden, yet I had perfect peace with the decision.

Bob and I had been active members of this church for five years. In addition to teaching Sunday school, I sang in the choir, spoke at the ladies meetings, worked with the missions program, and continued in the Wednesday morning prayer meeting with Judy and Marge. I was happy at this church, and so was Bob.

In addition to activities within the church, I went to

Bible studies that met in homes like the one I had visited five years previously at Sandy's house. I had made a few close friends through Bible study gatherings. It was among these ladies that I met some who purported to be Spirit-filled. I considered myself Spirit-filled since I had accepted Jesus as my Savior. I felt confident of my salvation and was only inquisitive regarding the experience of what they called speaking in tongues. My own study of the Scriptures convinced me that speaking in tongues was, if anything, an optional experience.

A large church about two miles from our house advertised being Spirit-filled. Out of curiosity, I decided to visit it. Missing a Sunday morning service was out of the question for me. I knew the Scriptures well enough by this time to understand that I needed to be faithful to my home church first and foremost. Sunday evenings, however, were low-key and brief. Bob didn't mind if I visited the other church on a Sunday evening, although he had no desire to go along.

I drove into the parking lot of the big church and watched other people arriving to see what door they used. It was a metal building but large enough to seat one thousand to fifteen hundred people. Before getting out of the car, I said a short prayer: "Lord Jesus, I don't know about this Spirit-filled doctrine. If this is not of You, give me discernment and keep me from deception."

I followed a small crowd through a door and stood at the back of the assembly to scout a place to sit. An usher came and directed me to a pew that was halfway down the side aisle and on the left. With some shifting of positions, the practically full row made room for one more, and I took a seat next to a lady on the end.

The service was in full swing as the congregation sang praise choruses in full, rich volume. The choruses were displayed on a screen at the front so that everyone, including visitors, could join in the singing. I instantly liked the upbeat music and the beautiful words of praise. Joining with them in song was easy, and I sang praises to the Lord with all of my heart.

The tempo changed, and the congregation sang a lilting chorus in rounds and broke into harmony. As I heartily sang unto the Lord, I burst into tears. Clamping my hand over my mouth, I muffled the sound and ducked down, trying not to draw attention to myself.

The lady sitting next to me couldn't miss my response. She leaned over to me and whispered, "That's the Holy Spirit, honey. Are you filled with the Spirit?"

I was crying too hard to answer so she asked another question: "Have you ever spoken in tongues?"

I shook my head to express no. "That's why you're crying," she said. "You are feeling the Spirit but do not have the gift of tongues as an outlet to express your feelings."

When the singing ended, I dried my eyes and straightened up to listen to the preaching. This was the part I was waiting for. Having come out of false doctrine and deception, I was leery, to say the least, of anything and everything. I viewed the written Word of God as my final authority and rod of discernment.

The minister stepped to the pulpit and announced, "Now we will pray in our prayer language."

Hands went up all over the building. Faces were lifted, and everyone began speaking in tongues at once. I sat still and watched and listened with interest. I don't know about this, I thought to myself. Is this for real?

I could not hear any one person in particular. There were too many people, and they were all praying simultaneously. The noise filled the room, but it was a rather pretty sound. In the same manner as they had all begun speaking in tongues, they all stopped. That was it. The preacher began his sermon.

I listened intently to the preaching, but something didn't sound right about it. The preacher was talking about prosperity and positive thinking. I had the distinct impression that God was viewed as a butler to do their bidding and answer their demands. I was unimpressed; I left.

The following Sunday, I caught my pastor in the hall. He was standing off to the side and looked unhurried, so I took the opportunity to ask his thoughts on speaking in tongues and what it means to be Spirit-filled. This quiet, unassuming man did not hesitate to tell me that he did not have a full understanding of the growing numbers of people claiming to have spoken in an unknown language. He did state, however, that believers are given different gifts of the Spirit and that speaking in tongues is not for everyone. I respected his candor in admitting that he didn't have all the answers.

More than desiring to speak in tongues, I was inquisitive about the subject for the purpose of having understanding. A cloak of confusion spurred me to search for answers until I had the peace that comes with understanding. I had no intention or desire to change churches. The clarity of the Scriptures was my goal.

In my daily prayers, I presented my questions to the Lord. Another gem from Ruth was the teaching about answers from God: He always answers. He may say yes or no, but sometimes His answer is to wait. The Lord did not answer my questions right away. I continued to lay questions before Him and knew that, in His time, the understanding would come.

While I was waiting for answers from the Lord, another development took place that brought more questions. Steadfast feeding on God's Word for five years had the benefit of placing in my heart and mind unfathomed potential to grow in the grace and knowledge of the Lord Jesus Christ, learn doctrine, be reproved, and receive correction in righteousness.

On my knees one morning in prayer, a phrase from the Old Testament came to my mind and I repeated it out loud: "Hear, O Israel: The LORD our God is one LORD" (Deuteronomy 6:4).

What does that mean? I wondered. Why did that verse of Scripture come to my mind?"

For the next six months, the same verse of Scripture would surface in my mind and became part of my daily prayers. Since it was a short verse, I simply stated it and then went on with my praying. The Lord will give me understanding of that verse of Scripture too, I thought. He doesn't do things without a reason.

During that six months, I continued withdrawing from activities at church. I loved being in the choir, and I was as surprised as anybody else when I not only quit the choir but desired to quit. I called Marge and Judy and told them I needed a sabbatical from the Wednesday morning prayer meeting. "I'm sure that I will join back with you," I told Marge. "There are many things in my mind that I do not understand right now. I am on hold with the Lord, and I am waiting to see what's going to happen next."

My doorbell rang, and I opened the door to a beautiful middle-aged saleswoman. I invited her in and looked at her brochures while we talked. The longer I looked at her, the more I began to notice that her beauty was out of the ordinary. Her features were ordinary, and yet, something about her gave the impression of beauty.

There's seems to be a glow about her. And her hair is beautiful, I thought as I looked at the flowing blond mane that reached below her waist. Her fair complexion had a pink hue from walking in the fresh air for door-to-door sales. Her face was clean without a trace of makeup, and she was dressed attractively in a skirt and blouse.

She talked easily and dispelled any shyness on my part, so I asked for her name. "Helen," she replied with a bright smile.

Turning my attention back to the brochures, Helen carried on animated conversation. The phrase "blessings of the Lord" caused me to look up from the booklets. "Oh, you know the Lord?"

"I sure do," she quickly replied.

Talking about the Lord always sparks my interest, and I can often tell within minutes or seconds if another person is open for discussion on my favorite subject—Jesus and His written Word. Helen was open. My first tentative questions were met with hearty and cheerful responses.

"How fun! I've met someone who likes to talk about the Lord as much as I do," I said to Helen with excitement. During the next two hours I discovered another unusual characteristic about Helen. She knew the Scriptures well. Few people do. In my five years of consistent daily Bible reading, Ruth's words were coming to pass. I was learning quickly and growing in the grace and knowledge of the Lord Jesus Christ. The Word of God was teaching me how to live from day to day. Once I started reading the Bible, I stayed in it. I had found answers to staying married, raising children, why there is suffering in the world, how to cope, and how to keep hope and faith burning in my heart. Why would I ever want to quit reading it?

" . . . the Holy Ghost," Helen was saying.

"You are one of those Spirit-filled people," I said, "like that church down the road a couple of miles from here."

"No, not like them," Helen said.

"What's the difference?" I inquired.

"Why don't you come and see for yourself?"

"I go to my own church on Sunday mornings," I told her.

"We have a ladies prayer meeting on Wednesday mornings. Come with me."

"I'd love to! I've been meeting with ladies for prayer on Wednesday mornings for five years."

We made arrangements to meet on Wednesday, and I wrote out a small order from the booklet Helen had given me. Helen was about ready to go, but I was drawn to her like a magnet. Her knowledge of the Bible far surpassed mine, and I wanted to soak from her like a sponge.

I commented on her beautiful hair, especially the length of it. Most women want their hair short enough to blow-dry and be on their way with a busy schedule. I felt that way too, but the beauty of Helen's hair was captivating.

"I never cut it," she said.

"Never?" I said incredulously. "What do you do with split ends? Why don't you cut it?"

"It's in the Bible," Helen stated without hesitation.

"I've never seen that. Show me," I was just as quick to say.

I brought my Bible to Helen and sat beside her. She opened to I Corinthians chapter eleven and read the whole chapter to me.

"I've read that many times, Helen, and I don't see where it says not to cut your hair."

"Look closely, Mary. It says for women to pray with their heads covered. Verse fifteen clearly states that the hair is the covering. Verse six says, 'If it be a shame for a woman to be shorn or shaven, let her be covered.' A careful study of this chapter shows that a woman's hair is not to be cut. The Bible does not say it has to be a certain amount of inches, because hair lengths will differ. The principle is to leave the hair long."

I sat still and looked closely at the verses in chapter eleven. "That's strange. I've never heard of such a thing. What's wrong with cutting our hair? I can't imagine why God would care about that."

"God does care. Look at verse thirteen: 'Judge in yourselves: is it comely that a woman pray unto God uncovered?' Verses seven through eleven tell the reason for it. This chapter is really talking about spiritual authority. Man is the image and glory of God, but woman is the glory of the man. God has delineated distinct roles for men and women."

"But you can't build a doctrine or principle on just one verse, Helen. People go astray by pulling out one verse of Scripture and making it say what they want."

"This isn't one verse, Mary. It's a whole chapter. It must be important to God since He devoted much of an entire chapter to it. God cares how we look and dress. He wants our bodies covered, and the male and female roles distinct. Look in Deuteronomy chapter twenty-two, verse five: 'The woman shall not wear that which pertaineth unto a man, neither shall a man put on a woman's garment: for all that do so are abomination unto the LORD thy God.'"

Helen turned to that verse of Scripture and let me read it for myself. "Notice the words 'abomination unto the LORD.' God never changes. If something was an abomination to Him thousands of years ago, it still is today. That's why I wear skirts and dresses. Pants pertain unto a man."

"But, Helen, there are many pants made for women that are feminine in style and fabric."

"Suppose I made a dress out of masculine fabric, Mary. Would your husband wear it?"

"No, he wouldn't, and I wouldn't want him to either. It would look funny."

"That's what everyone used to think about women wearing pants. It's only because the system of the world has desensitized people that they no longer think it is strange. Mary, these things won't make a lot of sense to you until you are filled with the Holy Ghost. The Bible says, 'The things of God knoweth no man, but the Spirit of God' (I Corinthians 2:11). Come with me Wednesday and you will learn more."

"I thought that I was filled with God's Spirit because I accepted Jesus as my Savior. Are you saying that I'm not?"

"Mary, you *do* have a walk with God, but there is more for you. Come with me Wednesday."

"I'm scared, Helen. I've been deceived before, and I don't want to be deceived again. I have to see everything in Scripture and not just in one place. Just keep showing me Scripture. It's the only thing I trust. One of my favorite verses is, 'Let God be true, but every man a liar' (Romans 3:4)."

It was hard for me to let Helen leave. I knew I could no longer detain her. She had already stayed long enough to disrupt her schedule. Jennifer was coming in from school as I said goodbye to Helen.

"Who was that, Mom?"

"A saleslady that I met today. She knows the Lord and the Bible. I wanted to talk to her for hours. Did you think she was pretty, Jennifer?"

"She sure had long hair," Jennifer remarked.

"Come on, Jen. Let's go look out my bedroom window and see if we can see her again."

We ran to the bedroom together. At eleven years old, Jennifer was almost as tall as I was. She could easily see out of the window even though it was high on the wall. I pushed back the curtain, and we strained to catch a glimpse of Helen as she walked to the next house. "Maybe she went the other way," I said.

"No, there she is, Mom. She's heading for the front door at Patsy's house."

"Yes, I see her. Jennifer, what is it about her? Does she strike you as beautiful too?"

"I guess it's that hair. I've never seen hair that long, but it is pretty. I don't think I want mine that long, Mom. It must be hard to take care of it."

"She said strange things, Jennifer. But she knew the Bible as well as Ruth. In fact, I think she knew the Bible better than Ruth, and I've *never* met anyone before who knew the Bible better than Ruth."

Jennifer went to change into play clothes, and I tried to figure out why I was so eager to visit Helen's church.

Chapter Fifteen

The Presence

The day after I met Helen, she came back and brought her pastor's wife, whom she referred to as Sister Barnett. I welcomed them both into my living room. Immediately, I was struck with the same impression of beauty that I had seen in Helen as I looked at Sister Barnett. She too had beautiful blond hair, but hers was arranged in curls in an upswept fashion. A disciplined lifestyle was evidenced by her trim figure dressed in a navy skirt with a red belt and a crisp white blouse. With the wisdom and grace that comes with fifty years of living for God, Sister Barnett evoked the unmistakable image of elegance, a woman to be honored and respected.

Helen had been on my mind since my meeting her the previous day, and I was glad she came to visit and brought this gracious lady. Sister Barnett spoke evenly and calmly. "Helen told me about you and your hunger for God's Word. I wanted to come and meet you. She has invited you to our Wednesday prayer meeting. I do hope you will come."

We only visited a few minutes. I assured them that I would be at the prayer meeting. Sister Barnett handed me a small book as they were leaving. It was entitled *Is Jesus in the Godhead or the Godhead in Jesus?* by Gordon Magee.

"I wish you could stay longer," I stated hopefully as I took the book from Sister Barnett.

"No, we must be going," she answered firmly.

Later, I understood the wisdom of Sister Barnett's timing. She did not get into debatable discussions with me. She simply gave me of her time and left me with something to read and pray about on my own. She trusted the Lord to do the rest.

That night, I sat on the couch with Gordon Magee's book. It only took about an hour to read it, but what an hour that was. The book was doctrinal and took the stance that there is one God and His name is Jesus. The thesis was that Jesus was fully God and fully man.

I read the book in its entirety because Mr. Magee used only Scripture to document his thesis, showing that Jesus is God in the flesh. He kept to the rule of explaining Scripture with Scripture, going from Genesis to Revelation to explain the oneness of God.

At first, I was reading from an objective viewpoint but with interest. He explained that the Bible never once says that Jesus is in the Godhead but states the opposite, that the Godhead is in Jesus. "For in him ["him" is seen to be Christ by looking at the verse above it] dwelleth all the fulness of the Godhead bodily" (Colossians 2:9).

Another verse I carefully studied was Isaiah chapter

nine verse six: "For unto us a child is born, unto us a son is given: and the government shall be upon his shoulder: and his name shall be called Wonderful, Counsellor, The mighty God, The everlasting Father, The Prince of Peace."

Obviously Isaiah was referring to Jesus, because the verse speaks of a child being born and a son being given. The titles given in the remainder of the verse attribute the Son, Jesus, with being not only Wonderful and the Counselor of all counselors, but also with being the mighty God and the everlasting Father.

This was shocking news to me. The trinitarian view was what I had been taught and thought throughout my life. Skeptically, I kept reading. The Scriptures were powerful, and when I put the book down, I had a similar feeling inside as I had when I was crossed by Mardel. I felt a ripping inside as my beliefs were uprooted yet again.

Bob was sitting on the love seat next to the couch reading the newspaper. I handed the book to him and said, "See what you think about this."

He gave a cursory glance at the title and tossed it on the end table. "Okay, I'll read it later."

I could tell by his response that he had not taken me seriously. "Bob, I *need* you to read that book. I need your input. It talks about one God instead of a trinity. My problem is that it's convincing and that scares me. Everybody knows there's a trinity! Please read it and help me decipher the content."

Bob looked up from his newspaper. I stood up and came closer to show how important it was to me. "You think so logically, and you're not overly emotional. Please read it and help me discern truth from error."

"I didn't realize how important it was to you. I'll read it and let you know," he promised.

Breathing a sigh of relief, I went to the bedroom to pray. "Lord, what's happening now? Surely I can't be wrong again, especially about something so basic as the trinity. This makes no sense to me. It's that same feeling I had five years ago when Mardel told me I was wrong. I never thought I would have to go through that experience again. Lord, there *has* to be a trinity. Too many people believe it; it's common knowledge. There are many verses of Scriptures that make sense with the trinitarian doctrine. How do You explain those?"

"Study to shew thyself approved unto God, a workman that needeth not to be ashamed, rightly dividing the word of truth," came the answer to my mind. I recognized it as a verse found in second Timothy chapter two. It was verse fifteen.

"I will study, Lord. I know the importance of studying Your Word without preconceived notions. It never occurred to me that the trinity could be a preconceived notion. *You* show me, Lord. Show me in Your Word. You'll have to be clear on this one, Lord. The doctrine of the trinity is too important to treat trivially."

I had a lot to study and pray about for the next few days. Wednesday came quickly, and I still wanted to visit Helen's church. It was ten or twelve miles from my house, so Helen met me halfway and drove the rest of the way. Being unfamiliar with the back roads, I could easily have gotten lost trying to find it alone.

Pearland Tabernacle looked octagon shaped from the front. The foyer was warmly decorated with gold-leaf wallpaper. Two high-back velvet chairs were separated by a small table holding a flower arrangement. A large gold-framed mirror brightened the wall above the table. Plaques of merit for giving to missions and other needs hung on the opposite walls, revealing the generous spirit of the church members.

Hallways surrounded the main sanctuary, which was located in the center. The Sunday school rooms, kitchen, and fellowship hall were in the back of the building. Helen took me into the sanctuary. It was capable of seating six or seven hundred people comfortably. Helen pointed to a door on the left. "That door goes into the men's prayer room," she explained. Pointing to an identical door on the right she said, "That door opens to the ladies' prayer room."

Sounds were coming from the door on the right and became louder as we neared the room. Helen went in first, and I followed close behind. Twenty-five or thirty women were in various places and positions around the room. Some were kneeling, some were standing, but all of them were praying. I had never seen anything like it before in my life. Their prayers were fervent. They were praying as individuals but all at the same time.

Helen leaned toward me and whispered, "God can hear us all at once. He's big enough to handle it."

My knees started shaking. "Helen, what's going on in here? I feel something very powerful, like nothing I've ever felt before, not ever."

"It's okay, Mary. It's the presence of God. Don't be afraid of Him."

"I *am* afraid. I'm not so sure that this is God. There's no doubt, it's *something*."

Turning around would have taken too long. I just

started backing up until I was out the door. Helen came quickly to my side. I was moving away from that room.

"Helen, there is a supernatural power in there like I have never known, not even in the occult. I just want to know which *team* it is. I've *got* to know if it's of God or if it's a counterfeit by what the Bible calls familiar spirits. I've been deceived before. I can't bear to be in false doctrine again."

Sister Barnett came through the door and joined Helen at my side. Helen explained my fears to her.

"It is wise to be cautious, Mary," Sister Barnett counseled. "There is much counterfeit in the world today. You must remember, though, that the devil only counterfeits what is real. For example, you would not make a counterfeit six-dollar bill because a real six-dollar bill does not exist. It would be spotted immediately as fake. The devil is smart. He takes what is real and makes something so close to it that many people are deceived. The safety from deception comes from knowing the *real*. Counterfeit experts study the real in order to spot the fake. Likewise, we should study the *real*, which is the Bible, in order to discern the lies and tricks of the devil. The devil is 'a liar, and the father of it.' "

"I have been studying the Bible, Sister Barnett, for five years."

"The Lord has seen that, Mary. He is guiding you. The Bible says that the sheep know His voice and will follow after Him. It is the presence of God that you felt in the prayer room. It is not uncommon for people to tremble in His awesome presence. The children of Israel trembled at the foot of Mount Sinai. 'There were thunders and lightnings, and a thick cloud upon the mount, and the voice of the trumpet exceeding loud; so that all the people that was in the camp trembled' (Exodus 19:16)."

Sister Barnett was using the Scriptures to answer me. I liked that. It was still the only thing I would respond to. It took fifteen minutes for the two of them to talk me into going back into the prayer room. As I entered back in, Sister Barnett was telling the other ladies about my fears. She asked them to form a circle by holding hands and to pray together for me. I stood in the midst of them shaking like a leaf. The indescribable presence of power filled the room. I felt as if I were at the Superbowl as opposed to a high school football game.

Some of the ladies spoke in tongues, but this was very different from the church near my house. Here, they spoke in tongues "as the Spirit gave them utterance." There was no general announcement for everyone to speak in tongues simultaneously. What a difference!

Helen and I had a lot to discuss after the prayer meeting. She invited me to the Sunday evening service. I accepted, and the surprise on her face told me she had thought I would never come back.

I *had* to come back. I felt compelled to come back. It was as if there were a hook in my mouth pulling and reeling me in on a line. I had to find out what was in that room.

Chapter Sixteen

The Full Gospel

"Yo! Mom! Mother! Where are you?"

I could hear Jennifer calling for me from the front room of the house. "I'm back here in the closet, Jen!"

Bob and I had moved back into the master bedroom and put Jeffery in the front bedroom. Dwayne and Keven's mother had recently moved to Washington State, taking the two boys with her.

Jennifer came down the hall to the back bedroom and poked her head into the closet. "What are you doing in here, Mom?"

"I'm looking for a skirt. I know there is one in here somewhere." I continued pushing slacks and jeans aside as I went down the clothes rod to the back of the closet.

"I've been studying those verses Helen showed me. I want to wear a skirt today. Ah, here it is." I pulled out a royal blue wraparound skirt. "I knew I had a skirt here."

"Are you going to start wearing skirts all the time?" Jennifer asked.

"I don't know. Not for now. I'm just thinking about all of these things that I'm hearing and studying. Helen told me to take my time. That's what I want to do—take time to study it thoroughly. I'm going to the evening service tonight. Do you want to go with me?"

"No thanks. You check it out, Mom. You can tell me about it when you get back."

I went by myself that night and sat with Helen and her family. Like the Spirit-filled church near my house, this group started off with lively songs of praise also. There was no screen up front to display the words, though. I listened to the singing and watched the faces of the people. There was no announcement for everyone to speak in tongues after the singing. I remembered what I had heard in the ladies prayer room. The few who did speak in tongues were spontaneous, fervent, and powerful. These people are different, I thought to myself. There's something else different about them too, I pondered. I couldn't figure out what it was yet.

"Let's lift our hands and worship the Lord," Brother Barnett directed from the pulpit.

Lifting hands up in church was uncomfortable for me. I just watched the others. Looking from one face to another, I tried to discover what the other difference was that I was sensing. Eyes were closed on each face. Tears were on the cheeks of many. That's it! Look at the tears. This is *worship*! It goes beyond praise. It's deep, from their hearts, and that's what I want. I wonder what the preaching will be like. I've heard that these people only talk about their "experiences" in God and don't base much on the Bible. Helen certainly knows the Bible. I wonder about everyone else here.

My reverie was interrupted as Brother Barnett was saying that he would not be preaching that night. He had asked his son-in-law, Ken Gurley, to preach.

Brother Gurley was a young man in his late twenties. He was of medium height with a stocky build and broad shoulders. His brown hair was cut neatly and combed back. Wide-set brown eyes complemented his big smile.

"My sermon tonight is entitled 'Famine for the Word.' " Without a verbal cue, all stood to their feet when Brother Gurley opened his Bible. Helen whispered to me, "We always stand for the reading of the Scripture."

After reading his text, Brother Gurley directed the congregation to be seated. I was unprepared for what happened next. Never before had a sermon held my attention so intently. The boyish smile was gone from Brother Gurley's face. The man was transformed into a powerhouse, a dynamo, as Scripture after Scripture poured forth from him throughout the entire message. The sermon was going past my ears and reaching my heart. No sermon had ever done that before. I was too enthralled to ask Helen about it at the moment. I didn't want to miss a word.

The sermon ended too quickly for me. My mouth dropped open when I looked at my watch. He had been preaching for almost an hour. I had lost track of time.

People were moving to the altars at the front. Helen turned to me and asked, "Would you like to go forward and pray?"

"N-no thanks. I'll stay here."

Helen saw my obvious fright and put her hand over mine. "Helen, it's that same awesome power that I felt at your ladies prayer meeting. My knees are knocking."

"The Spirit of the Lord is moving in here, Mary. You can be filled with the Holy Ghost tonight."

"I don't understand that. I'm not ready for whatever you're talking about. I wish I could talk to the man who just preached. He used so much Scripture, and I have a lot of questions. I've never heard preaching like that. It was piercing."

"That's anointing," said Helen. "No man can conjure that up. Men can be humanly inspired, but only God can give an anointing."

"Helen, I'm too scared to go up there. I'm going to ask God to bring someone to me."

"Okay. I'll pray with you, Mary."

Helen and I closed our eyes and prayed together. We had been praying for three or four minutes when a familiar voice caused me to open my eyes. Sister Barnett had come back and was standing in front of me.

"She's too frightened to go up front, Sister Barnett," Helen said in my stead. "She has a lot of questions and would like to talk to Brother Gurley."

Sister Barnett smiled and said, "I can arrange that. Helen, take Mary to the church office. Brother Gurley and I will meet you there in a few minutes."

I was mortified. Helen's bold request brought about the meeting I wanted, but now my shy streak rose up, and I wanted to find a hole to crawl into and hide. "Helen, I can't talk to Brother Gurley. I don't even *know* him."

"I'm going with you, Mary. Sister Barnett will be there too. He can answer your myriad of questions. You have more questions than Quaker has oats. The Lord is providing a way for you to get answers. That's what we prayed for, isn't it? Come on. We can't keep them waiting."

There was nothing for me to do at that point but go with Helen. We went down the hall and into the office reception area. Brother Gurley was in one of the offices sitting behind a desk. He motioned for us to come in. Sister Barnett was already there sitting in a chair in front of the desk. She motioned to the other two chairs ready for me and Helen.

Brother Gurley greeted me, but his manner was intense. Oddly, his intensity did not make me more uncomfortable but rather made me feel that this was an important conversation. And it was.

Sizing up the situation, I fully recognized what Helen had tried to tell me. This was truly an opportunity to get answers. With that thought in mind, I overrode shyness and asked everything I could think of.

"What about tongues? The Bible says that not every one has the gift of tongues. To each person is given a different gift as the Spirit wills," I tossed out to him.

"That's in I Corinthians, Mary. That epistle is written to the church at Corinth. The people to whom the apostle Paul was writing were already filled with the Holy Ghost. The word 'gift' in Corinthians is from the Greek word *charisma.* It is true that not every believer has the gift, charisma, of tongues. But the gift of the Holy Ghost as evidenced by speaking in tongues is found in the Book of Acts. The word 'gift' in Acts 2:38 is from the Greek word *dorea.* This is *not* the same as the gift of tongues spoken of in Corinthians. Everyone who is filled with the Holy Ghost, or Holy Spirit, will speak in tongues. It's the sound of life from a newborn child of God."

Brother Gurley continued to speak, "Jesus said, in the Gospel of John, that *everyone* must be 'born of water and of the Spirit.' Jesus went on to say that just as the wind blows through the trees and you cannot tell from whence it comes but you can *hear* the sound thereof, so it is with *everyone* who is born of the Spirit. When you are born of the Spirit, you will hear the sound thereof. You will speak in tongues."

I looked at Brother Gurley. He was emphatic and unflinching. "I've been born again. I've accepted Jesus as my Savior."

"You must be born of the water and of the Spirit," came the rejoinder.

"I've been baptized in water. I was immersed, and besides, baptism is an outward symbol of an inward decision."

Brother Gurley's eyes were steady. "Jesus did not say baptism was an outward symbol. Jesus said you *must* be born of the water and of the Spirit."

"I thought it was a symbol, but the fact remains, I was baptized in water."

"How were you baptized? Was it in the name of Jesus or in the titles of Father, Son, and Holy Ghost?"

"Father, Son, and Holy Ghost," I answered. "I didn't know there was any other way."

"Let's look at the Scriptures," Brother Gurley said as he opened the Bible on his desk. He put his Bible in front of me and pointed to Matthew chapter twenty-eight, verse nineteen. I read the verse as he quoted it: "Go ye therefore, and teach all nations, baptizing them in the name of the Father, and of the Son, and of the Holy Ghost."

"Look at this word, Mary." Brother Gurley pointed to the word "name." "Notice that it is singular. That is very important. Now let's look at the other verses of Scripture referring to baptism."

He turned to Acts 2:38 and quoted as I read: "Then Peter said unto them, Repent, and be baptized every one of you in the name of Jesus Christ for the remission of sins, and ye shall receive the gift of the Holy Ghost."

"There are several things to notice in this verse, Mary. First, look at the words 'every one of you.' That doesn't sound like an option to me. It sounds like exactly what it says: every one is to be baptized. Peter does not make it optional; he is not merely suggesting that every one be baptized. Peter states, 'Be baptized.'

"Next, notice that Peter does not mention the titles of Father, Son, and Holy Ghost. Peter commands every one to be baptized in the name of Jesus. This agrees with the verse in Matthew, which says be baptized in the name of the Father, the Son, and the Holy Ghost. The name of the Father, Son, and Holy Ghost is Jesus.

"Then, notice that baptism is for the remission of sins. Again, it does not say it's for a symbol."

I interrupted Brother Gurley on that one. "The shedding of blood is for remission of sins according to Hebrews 9:22."

"Without shedding of blood is no remission," Brother Gurley quoted. "The blood of Jesus paid the price of death that our sin demands. That blood is applied in water baptism when the name of Jesus is invoked in faith. Look at Luke 24:47: 'And that repentance and remission of sins should be preached in his name among all nations.' Remission of sins is linked to the name of Jesus."

"Brother Gurley, you can't pull one verse out and make a doctrine. Acts 2:38 is only one verse."

"There are plenty more that say the same thing, Mary. Look at Acts 8:16, Acts 10:48, and Acts 19:5."

We looked at each verse together. They all taught the same thing: baptism in the name of Jesus. I had never seen it before. I was losing ground. "Why does Matthew say Father, Son, and Holy Ghost?"

Brother Gurley didn't lose patience with me. He explained it one more time, "In Matthew, the word 'name' is singular. Mary, you are a wife, a mother, and someone's daughter, but you are not three people and you only have one name. Jesus is Father in creation, Son in redemption, and Holy Ghost in regeneration, but He is not three persons and He only has one name. It's the name above all names, the name of Jesus. When you are baptized in the name of Jesus as Matthew, Peter, and Paul have written, you take on the name of Jesus. The church is called the bride of Christ. The bride takes the name of the groom. His name is not Father, Son, and Holy Ghost. His name is Jesus."

It was beginning to make sense to me. That was scary because it was new to me, and different from everything I had been taught. I couldn't argue with the Scriptures though. And Brother Gurley stuck with the Scriptures.

I knew a lot of Scriptures too, and another one popped into my mind. "What about Acts 16:30 and 31? The jailer asked Paul how to be saved, and Paul answered 'Believe on the Lord Jesus Christ, and thou shalt be saved, and thy house.' Looking at that verse, I would say that you are adding to the requirements of salvation, Brother Gurley."

"Mary, you stated earlier that one cannot pull a verse out of context and make a doctrine out of it. Now you are trying to do that yourself. Let's read the rest of that section in Acts chapter sixteen. Verse thirty-three tells us that after the jailer professed his belief in Jesus, he went the same hour of the night and was baptized. If a profession of faith is enough by itself and baptism is merely an outward symbol, then why did Paul take the jailer to be baptized in the middle of the night? What was the urgency, and who was the symbol for?"

I stared at the Scriptures in front of me. Past deception caused me to check every facet of information that I was reading and hearing. I threw another question back at him. "You are making a doctrine of works out of salvation. Paul said in Ephesians, 'For by grace are ye saved through faith; and that not of yourselves: it is the gift of God: not of works, lest any man should boast.' If I have to be baptized and speak in tongues to be saved, then you are adding works to belief."

With lightning quickness and accuracy, Brother Gurley quoted from the Book of James: " 'Even so faith, if it hath not works, is dead, being alone. . . . Faith without works is dead.' And Paul said in Philippians, 'Work out your own salvation with fear and trembling.' "

"That doesn't make sense. One can't be saved by grace through faith and at the same time work to be saved," I retorted.

Sister Barnett spoke in her calm voice from beside me, "We can't work to earn salvation, Mary; that's true. No one is good enough; we are saved by grace through faith in the precious blood of Jesus. Our faith will spark us, however, to do what is right. True faith will lead to obedience of the Scriptures. That is why the jailer went to be baptized that night. He had a saving faith, and he obeyed the teaching of Paul and was baptized. Obedience is not works. Obedience is faith in action, following after the Spirit. 'For as many as are led by the Spirit of God, they are the sons of God' (Romans 8:14). Anyone can *say* he believes in Jesus and then go live any way he pleases. That is not Bible salvation."

"That's right," Brother Gurley interjected. "Think about it, Mary. It agrees with Jesus' words that you must be born of the water and the Spirit. Can you see how all of the Scriptures line up without contradiction when you have the right understanding of them and don't pull one out of context?"

That feeling of panic began to rise in me. I looked at Sister Barnett. "Are you all saying that I'm not saved?"

"Here's another verse of Scripture," Brother Gurley was quick to say: " 'In flaming fire taking vengeance on them that know not God, and that obey not the gospel of our Lord Jesus Christ' (II Thessalonians 1:8)."

I looked at all three of them—Brother Gurley, Sister Barnett, and Helen. A frantic feeling of trying to keep the proverbial rug under my feet swept over me. "The gospel is the death, burial, and resurrection of the Lord Jesus Christ according to I Corinthians chapter fifteen, verses one through four," I announced to the three of them. "What does it mean to *obey* the gospel?"

Brother Gurley turned back to Acts chapter two, verse thirty-eight, and quoted it again, correlating it to the gospel, " 'Then Peter said unto them, Repent. . . .' Repentance is *death* to the self-life. One is more than sorry for his sins. He turns from sin and forsakes it. His life changes. 'I am crucified with Christ: nevertheless I live; yet not I, but Christ liveth in me' (Galatians 2:20). We are *buried* with Him in baptism. 'Therefore we are buried with him by baptism into death' (Romans 6:4). We are *resurrected* from our dead state of sin when we are quickened by His Spirit. 'And you hath he quickened, who were dead in trespasses and sins' (Ephesians 2:1). There you have it. We obey the gospel, which is Christ's death, burial, and resurrection, when we die to our sinful life, are buried with Him in baptism, and are raised to new life with Him by being filled with His Spirit. There are no contradictions."

By this time, I was thoroughly humbled by their knowledge of the Scriptures. There is a difference between knowing Scriptures as the sword of the Spirit and being skilled with that sword. Anyone can hold a knife, but a surgeon is skilled with the knife. The rug under my feet was definitely unraveling as Brother Gurley's skill with the sword of the Spirit cut away the traditions of men that I had previously accepted without question.

There was one more thread I had to have pulled. Praying that their patience with me would hold out, I mentioned Romans chapter ten, verse nine. "Brother Gurley, it says, 'If thou shalt confess with thy mouth the Lord Jesus, and shalt believe in thine heart that God hath raised him from the dead, thou shalt be saved.' "

"Keep reading, Mary," Brother Gurley urged.

I read out loud until he stopped me at verses fourteen, fifteen, and sixteen. They were familiar verses to me, but I was seeing them in a new light. This time I noticed the word "gospel." "And how shall they believe in him of whom they have not heard? and how shall they hear without a preacher? . . . But they have not all obeyed the gospel. For Esaias saith, Lord, who hath believed our report?"

"Most of your questions can be answered, Mary, just by reading further down the page. The verse you read exhorting us to confess belief in Jesus with our mouth hinges on the rest of the chapter that explains where that belief comes from. It comes from hearing the gospel preached and then obeying the gospel."

Brother Gurley was turning the pages again and said, "I will show you one more before we go. Look at Acts chapter eight. You can see Philip preaching to the Samaritans. There were miracles in verse six, deliverance from evil spirits and healings in verse seven, and joy in verse eight. These people became *believers,* verse twelve says. The Lord did not leave them with only miracles and believing, however. Verses sixteen and seventeen tell us that they were baptized in the name of the Lord Jesus; then Peter and John went to Samaria and laid hands on them, and they received the Holy Ghost."

I stared at the page. It was irrefutable. I sat still to let everything sink in. Sister Barnett spoke gently, "Mary, let Helen give you a home Bible study to help you put it all together. These are new thoughts for you, and sometimes it just takes a little time. The Lord will help you to understand it more clearly."

"He has in the past, Sister Barnett. I know I can trust Him, but it's very frightening to have my foundation ripped up again."

"Ah, but this time, Mary, you will build on that solid rock, Christ Jesus. Then your foundation will never again be destroyed."

"That's what's scary. I thought I *had* built on the rock Christ Jesus."

We all rose to leave as Sister Barnett quoted one more

verse: " 'He that believeth on me, as the *scripture hath said*, out of his belly shall flow rivers of living water,' (John 7:38). Many people profess belief in Jesus, but not according to what is proclaimed in the Bible."

I turned to leave and then turned back once more. "What changed my life five years ago? I am not the same person. My life *did* clean up."

"The Word of God changed your life," said Sister Barnett. "When you repented, your heart was opened to the Bible. The Lord has been working *with* you through His Word. Now He wants to be *in* you by filling you with His Spirit."

They had an answer for everything. They knew the Bible. I went home to think and pray.

Chapter Seventeen

Water and Spirit

The fight was on. It was me against . . . against . . . whom? Against *them*! Helen, Sister Barnett, and Brother Gurley along with that whole strange bunch over there. After all, I thought, everybody's been baptized with the titles Father, Son, and Holy Ghost. Everybody wears pants. Everybody cuts her hair. Those people are ridiculous.

The sound of the doorbell broke into my mental tirade. It was Helen. "Hi, Helen. Come in. I was just thinking about you."

"I came to see how you're doing, Mary."

"I've about decided to stay put at my own church. It's a lot easier. Your people are too narrow. The ways of God can't possibly be that narrow. How can anyone find the way if it's that obscure and difficult? I've been reading the Bible every day for a long time, and I've never before seen the things you and Brother Gurley and Sister Barnett showed me."

"You're right. It is narrow. It always has been. There were only eight people on Noah's ark," Helen replied.

Helen's answer jolted me. "That's true," I said as I reflected on it.

"Mary, are you only thinking about everything, or are you praying about it and looking in your Bible?"

"I've been looking in my Bible. I'm just having trouble believing what I'm seeing. I can't find any instances of anyone being baptized in the titles of Father, Son, and Holy Ghost in the Bible, yet we all get baptized that way."

"You won't find it in the Bible, Mary. It doesn't exist. There is not one verse of Scripture that says to baptize in the titles, nor is there one instance in the Bible of anyone being baptized in the titles."

"I feel confusion, Helen. Where did peace in my soul go?"

"What you are feeling is not confusion. It is conviction. You have seen the Word of God, and you need to obey it. Then peace will return."

"I'm miserable. I feel a battle is going on inside of me," I confessed.

"The choice is yours, Mary. The Lord shows us the way and leaves us to choose. If you turn back, the battle will simmer down, but you won't be happy. If you come forward and obey the Scriptures, peace will return."

Helen moved toward the door. "I have a lot to do today. I just dropped by to check on you."

When Helen left I grabbed my Bible and sat at the kitchen table. "Lord, please show me the truth about baptism. Give me understanding," I prayed.

I looked at Matthew 28:19 again, then I turned to the Book of Acts and looked up every instance of baptism.

The name, the name, the name—it was everywhere I looked, including the verse in Matthew. "I'm not fighting Helen, Sister Barnett, and Brother Gurley. I'm fighting You once again, Lord. Baptism in Your name is in Your Word as clear as crystal. I have to do it. I have to be rebaptized."

Helen's short visit was timely. I felt as if I were sitting on a fence and could fall either direction. I was beginning to lean towards what I thought was the safe and easy direction when Helen's words yanked me back to the other side.

For the rest of the day I thought on the Scriptures referring to baptism and lay awake that night thinking and praying about them. By morning I had made a decision and picked up the phone.

The church phone was answered by Brother Barnett. "When can I be baptized in Jesus' name?" I asked him. "I've been reading about it since meeting with Brother Gurley a few days ago. I can't fight it anymore. It's in there."

Brother Barnett's hearty voice boomed back, "It sure is in there! I'm thrilled that you see it. We will be glad to baptize you in our next church service."

"Oh, no! I want to be baptized today. The Bible says I have to be born of the water and of the Spirit. I don't want to go one day if there is even a slight possibility that I'm not saved."

"Now that's what I like to hear," he responded. "What time would you like to come?"

Full of exuberance I said, "I can be there in twenty minutes."

Brother Barnett laughed. "How about one o'clock this

afternoon," he suggested. "That will give us time to call a few ladies to come and pray and rejoice with you at your baptism."

"Okay. I'll be there at one."

Brother and Sister Barnett along with Helen and a couple of her friends were waiting for me when I arrived. Helen gave me a baptismal robe and a large towel. When I was ready, we joined the others in the baptistery.

"The water's cold today, Mary," Brother Barnett warned me.

He wasn't kidding. It was teeth-chattering cold, but I didn't mind. "I want to be ready to meet Jesus face to face, so cold water is inconsequential. Let's go!"

Brother Barnett began to pray, and the ladies joined in with him praising and worshiping the Lord. I forgot about the cold water and held my nose. Brother Barnett immersed me, saying, "I baptize you in the lovely name of the Lord Jesus Christ for the remission of your sins," and brought me back up out of the water.

I lifted my hands and worshiped the Lord with the others. "You can receive the Holy Ghost right now," I heard one saying, but I wasn't ready for that. I brought my hands back down and climbed up the steps into the big, warm towel that Helen was holding up for me.

"For the remission of sins," I pondered as I dried and dressed.

"Helen, the Lord quickened a verse to me several months ago. It was Isaiah 59:2: 'But your iniquities have separated between you and your God, and your sins have hid his face from you, that he will not hear.' I was surprised that it leaped out at me when I read it because I didn't feel separated from God since I accepted Jesus as my Savior and was living for Him."

Helen handed me a hair dryer and a comb. "The Lord was preparing you for this baptism, Mary. Think of sin as a large burden strapped on your back. The price of sin, which is death, was paid for by the death of Jesus. Today, that baggage was cut loose from you when you went through the waters of baptism in the name of Jesus. Remember the children of Israel when they were crossing the Red Sea? The Egyptians, their enemies, were drowned in that sea. 'And were all baptized unto Moses in the cloud and in the sea' (I Corinthians 10:2). Your past can't follow you anymore, Mary. It's all washed away."

I smiled. "I believe it, Helen, and I thank God."

After being baptized, I did feel more at peace, but there were still many unanswered questions to be studied. I wanted to get an unbiased opinion, or even line up opposing views and lay them out before God. That had been effective when Mardel had set up an absolute.

Finding an opposing view was no problem. I went to my own church and my own pastor. The secretary informed me that he was on the phone, so I waited in the foyer. As I stood there, the youth minister passed by in the hallway.

"Hi, Mary! What are you up to?"

"I'm waiting for the pastor. He's on the phone."

"Is there anything that I can help you with?"

"I have some doctrinal questions. I want to see what he thinks and maybe if he has any books I can read."

"There are plenty of doctrinal books in my office. Why don't you come see if there is something I have that can help you?"

"What particular subjects do you need?" he asked as

he approached the bookshelves that lined the wall behind his desk.

"The trinity and the gift of tongues."

"The trinity?"

"Uh huh. I've run into this bunch of people that say there is no trinity. They baptize in Jesus' name and they speak in tongues."

The youth minister nodded in understanding. "My grandmother believed in all of that. She went to a church in Pearland."

"You have *got* to be kidding!" I exclaimed in surprise. "That's the church I have visited. Do you mean that you know about this odd doctrine?"

"Oh, I know about it all right. I looked into it myself."

"What happened?"

"I couldn't come to terms with the oneness they taught. I just couldn't see it," he answered.

"I've never heard of these things before in my life, and I'm thirty-two years old. Now I want to study it thoroughly and see if these things are true, but I don't trust those people. I want to read from both camps and then ask God what *He* thinks and study His Word. What have you got among your books?"

"Here are some excellent books from the seminary. I'll help you find your subjects," said the minister.

He turned and began reading material about the trinity. I was in for another shock. His own seminary book stated that the word *trinity* is mentioned no place in the Bible and that it is a total mystery that no one can comprehend or explain.

I stared at the open page of the thick book. "Look, can you believe that? That's your own book!"

A chair was nearby and I took a seat. "This is beyond my wildest imaginations. I wonder what your books say about baptism. Would you look that up?"

"Sure, let me see here." His fingers ran past several books on the shelf, and then he pulled one out and turned to the reference on baptism.

"According to this, the earliest mode of baptism was by immersion and in the name of Jesus. It was not until many years later that the titles Father, Son, and Holy Ghost were used."

A gasp came from my mouth. "You have *got* to be kidding!" I said again. "Listen, how can you ignore this? I am amazed that you know about it, and now your own books back it up. What are you going to do?"

"I'm not going to do anything," he responded. "I've given this a lot of thought quite some time ago. I'm not interested in looking back into it."

"This is only the beginning for me. I am flabbergasted."

"What are *you* going to do, Mary?"

"I'm going to the Houston library, that's what I'm going to do. Thanks for helping me look in your books."

The reference section was situated in the middle of the library. At my request the librarian directed me to the religious encyclopedias and dictionaries. I began pouring over the information in the huge volumes. The results were astonishing. Reference after reference stated that the early church knew nothing of a trinity. The doctrine of a trinity developed over a period of three hundred years and was formally accepted at the Council of Nicea in A.D. 325.

I pushed back from the study table to take a small

break. The library was quiet since it was midday. Young people were still in school, and most moms were at work. There was one woman in a nearby aisle perusing books. I started to bypass her but did a doubletake. She was wearing a dress and had very long dark hair. Her face was clean without a trace of makeup. She might be one of *them*, I thought. She dresses like the ladies at Helen's church.

I went over to her. "Excuse me. Are you by any chance one of those Pentecostals?"

"Yes, I am. I go to Pearland Tabernacle."

"You're *kidding*!" I exclaimed to her as I had done to the youth minister. It seemed to be my phrase for the day. "I visited there, and today I'm studying about the doctrine. Would you come talk with me for a few minutes?"

She came to the table where I had been studying, and we each took a seat while she told me that her name was Cheryl. I showed her the pages I had been reading and told her about the youth minister at my church. She had a relaxed manner and reinforced my line of study with confidence.

"I saw baptism in Jesus' name clearly in the Bible and was baptized by Brother Barnett," I told her. "Now I'm studying trinity versus oneness and looking up historical references on baptism. I also want to know more about the Holy Ghost."

"The Holy Ghost is for you," Cheryl said.

"I think I'm ready to pray about it, but the way they pray at Pearland Tabernacle is too strange for me. I can't pray like that."

"You can receive the gift of the Holy Ghost any place," she said.

"I can?"

"You can get it here in the library. You can get it at home. You can get it anywhere."

My hand came up to my face. "Not here!"

Cheryl laughed. "I'm just trying to tell you how easy it is. When you have repented and been baptized, it's a promise for you. You'll get it."

She stood up to go.

"Thanks for spending time with me. Maybe I'll see you at the church the next time I visit."

"I'll look for you," Cheryl said.

Cheryl left, and I put away the volumes and books. I had to be home before Jennifer and Jeffery came in from school.

During the next three weeks, another battle ensued in my mind and heart. I was drawn to the people at the Pentecostal church who were so full of God's Word. I kept looking at the Scriptures they had shown me and praying for understanding. If these people were right, I would have to leave the church I had come to love and the friends that I had made. My husband was not interested in the reports I had given him about my visits and studies concerning the people who taught one God, the gift of the Holy Ghost, and baptism in Jesus' name. I would have to go alone to this new church, leaving family, friends, and everything familiar to me.

The Lord reminded me of Abraham, whose profound faith in the unseen God moved him to pull up his tent stakes and leave Ur of the Chaldees. Abraham left everything that was familiar to him. I continued visiting Pearland Tabernacle on Sunday nights, and each service was powerful, filled with God's Word, and touched me in the core of my being.

One Sunday night, I made a decision. "Jesus, I choose You above everything and everyone. I know Your voice, and I *will* follow after You. I cannot see down the road where this will lead, but I can see right in front of me. Your Word is a lamp unto my feet. Right now I can only see one thing to do at a time. I will obey You at each step, and You will take care of the rest. I love You, Lord, because You first loved me."

Before I left for home, Helen talked to me about a Bible study. "Can I see the book?" I asked her.

Thumbing through it, I saw that it started in Genesis with Adam and Eve and went through Revelation, explaining prophecies concerning the end times. "This looks like a good Bible study, but I can't sit through weeks of Adam and Eve. I want to know more about being filled with the Holy Ghost."

"We'll get there, Mary. It's good to start from the beginning."

"I'm sure it is, but I can't do it that way right now. If you run across somebody who has never read the Bible, you could probably start with Adam and Eve, but I have to learn more about this Holy Ghost you all talk about. In fact, why don't you just let me borrow the book?"

Helen hesitated. "I promise to call you if I have any questions," I assured her until she relented.

I devoured the midsection of the book that night. Two things caught my attention. One was the instruction to *ask* for the filling of the Holy Ghost. "How much more shall your heavenly Father give the Holy Spirit to them that ask him?" (Luke 11:13). The other was the thought that the Holy Ghost is the quickening power that will catch a person up in the Rapture, sparing him from the wrath that is to come upon this world. That did it. I was ready to ask God to fill me with His Spirit.

The house was quiet. It was past eleven o'clock, and my family was already asleep. I turned off the lamp and looked around the living room. There was a tall shelving unit on each side of the fireplace. The one on the right had a thirty-gallon aquarium on the middle shelf. Its light was still on, giving off a glow in the area of the shelves and surrounding floor space.

I knelt on the floor in the small circle of light. Closing my eyes, I whispered to the Lord so that I wouldn't wake up Bob or the children. "Lord, I want to be filled with Your Spirit. I thought that I was filled, but if there is more for me, I would like to have it. I don't know how this works, because I've never seen anyone receive the Holy Ghost. You will have to tell me what to do. But before You do that, there is something I want to do. I must be sure that it's You, Lord, and not the other team. It's You that I want, Jesus, and no one else. I want the One who died on the cross for me. I want the God of Abraham, Isaac, and Jacob. I bind up any lying spirits that would try to deceive me right now. I don't want anything false. Jesus, You see my heart. You wouldn't bring me this far and then deceive me. I trust You. Thank You for forgiving my sins and washing them away. I want to live for You."

With more fervency I said, "I really want Your Spirit, Lord. I will wait all night if I have to."

An hour passed as I intermittently talked to the Lord and waited in silence for instructions. I looked at the clock. It was almost twelve-thirty.

I got up for a drink of water thinking, Well, maybe I won't wait all night.

After getting a drink in the kitchen, I paused a moment to decide what to do. Suddenly I made a firm decision. "I *will* wait. So what if it takes all night. This lady is going to be Rapture ready!"

I went back to my small circle of light and knelt once again. "I'm back, Lord. I'm here to stay. I want to be filled with Your Spirit, and I'm not moving until I am."

Moments ticked away in silence as I waited. "What do I do now, Lord?" I whispered.

"Praise," came to my mind.

"That's a good idea. I will praise You. Hallelujah! Glory to Your name, Jesus! Praise the Lord!" I whispered emphatically.

I lifted my hands and my face and kept praising the Lord. Thoughts began to come rapidly in my mind, words that I felt an urging to pray, compelled to pray. "Hallelujah!" I said again, but this time I felt a quickening power behind it.

"Come and fill me with Your Spirit, Lord," I found myself saying.

Unexpectedly, a small warfare began in my mind. It was almost as if there were two voices. One urged me on, and the other began to criticize me, saying, "What do you think you're doing? You have the Spirit. You don't need to do this. You had better stop this. This isn't necessary."

I had to push past the criticisms and doubts. "Maybe I don't need to do this, but I'm going to find out tonight for sure," I countered.

Words of praise were pouring into my mind also. I went with that voice and kept worshiping, "Glory, glory, hallelujah!"

Another change came abruptly. The words of praise began to flow like a stream. With my eyes still closed, my attention became riveted upward. A Presence descended over me and all around me. My surroundings seemed distant. I became totally focused and felt as if I had gone into a tunnel. Fear gripped me, and I considered backing off completely, but a previous thought returned to my mind. "You wouldn't bring me this far and lie to me. This has to be You, Jesus. I trust You."

My breathing became rapid and words were flowing fast. "Come and fill me with Your Spirit. I love You, Jesus."

My mouth and chin went numb, so numb that it felt I had received novacaine from the dentist. I whispered the next words that came to my mind. "Let it go."

As soon as I said those words, my tongue took off on its own. I lost all control of it. It was moving with incredible speed in my mouth, for seconds or minutes—I do not know how long—but when it stopped, I knelt there with my hands still up and tears streaming down my face.

I didn't want to move. I was totally enveloped in His Presence. In utter awe, I cried out quietly, "I've been touched by God, the God of the whole universe. You came to my living room. You came to me, personally."

I leaned forward from my knees until my forehead touched the floor and cried as I was bathed in His Presence. The clock was insignificant; I wanted to stay forever in His glorious embrace. "O, God, You are more real than I ever imagined," I whispered. "I have longed to be loved all of my life, and tonight I feel Your love for me like a well of water springing up in my heart and soul. I will never be the same again."

His Presence began to lift. Part of a verse of Scripture came to my mind and I spoke it from a heart filled to overflowing: "Thanks be unto God for his unspeakable gift" (II Corinthians 9:15).

Chapter Eighteen

Bob

Joy unspeakable and full of glory was resounding in my soul. I awoke with a smile on my face and a song in my heart. I was stopped short with the thought, Uh oh. Should I tell Bob what happened last night? He's going to think I'm crazy.

The answer was rapid in coming: "Whosoever shall deny me before men, him will I also deny before my Father which is in heaven" (Matthew 10:33).

"That settles it. I'll tell Bob."

Bob usually called me from his office during the day, so I waited for his call, which came about midmorning. I asked how he was doing and anticipated the question in reverse to relate my excitement to him. When he asked how I was doing, I worked momentarily to keep my voice calm and then replied, "I have some news to share with you. I received the Holy Ghost last night and spoke in tongues."

There was a pause on the other end of the line. Then

my ever-calm husband smoothly asked, "Really? What was it like?"

"It was great! Bob, you know that you and I have both believed that we had the Lord's Spirit in us by accepting Jesus as our Savior. Well, I can now say that there is definitely more to it than that. The difference is like looking at the cardboard picture of Mrs. Smith's pie on the carton versus eating the pie inside. No matter how much you study that cardboard, it can never amount to the joy and experience of eating and tasting the pie. Oh, taste and see that the Lord is good! It's wonderful!"

"So how did this experience happen?" he persisted in his placid line of questioning.

"I asked God to fill me with His Spirit, and I asked Him to help me pray. I waited and prayed for an hour or more, and then I felt this awesome Presence surround me. I was worshiping the Lord, and my tongue just took off. It was going so fast. I remember thinking that I can talk a lot sometimes, but even I can't talk that fast. It was incredible, indescribable, and glorious."

"Well, that sounds interesting," was all that he had to say.

The subject changed and I silently prayed, "Lord, this is another case for You to handle."

I proceeded to tell my children, my sisters, my neighbors, and anybody who would listen. The children took the news in stride, the neighbors had various reactions ranging from "That's fine for you, but leave me alone" to downright rejection, and my sisters were curious and wanted to know more about it.

"I'm studying and learning," I told my sisters. "So far, these Pentecostals have proven to be right."

"You keep studying and let us know," my sisters enjoined.

No prodding was needed. I was, as the apostle Paul said, apprehended by God. I could only go forward. On Sunday nights, I regularly went to church in Pearland. Bob was agreeable as long as I spent Sunday mornings with him in what had been our home church.

Jennifer started going with me on Sunday evenings. She liked the jubilant praise and worship. She had her twelfth birthday and was old enough to watch and listen and think. She was at a crucial age, and I asked the Lord for wisdom to answer her questions. I knew that she was old enough to teach but that it would be unwise to push, so I brought her with me and let her hear the preaching of the Word.

Within three short months, Jennifer was filled with the Holy Ghost. She became as excited as I was to get to church on Sunday nights. Even though the services lasted long, we both enjoyed them to the hilt. Often, when we arrived home at ten or ten thirty, we would be singing and skipping down the sidewalk to the front door. Then we would pause to compose ourselves and try to walk into the house nonchalantly. It never worked. We couldn't wipe the smiles from our faces.

Bob invariably asked, "How was it?"

We invariably answered, "It was great!"

Bob didn't ask for more details, but gradually I began to change, and he was circumstantially confronted with the changes. My inward joy was being reflected outwardly as my appearance became more and more separated from the dictates of the world.

The Scriptures' teaching uncut hair on women

instigated a small skirmish in my mind. Six months prior to meeting Helen, I had acquired a new haircut that made my frizzy hair manageable. My hair was off my shoulders for the first time in my adult life and was cut in layers. The layering helped to thin it and made it easy to use a circular brush and a blow dryer to smooth it and control it.

It should have been enough for me to have seen the Scriptures and then obey them, but I resisted the thought of losing my new hairdo. One night while driving home from a Sunday evening service, I put the question to the Lord again, "Do You really care what length my hair is?"

I was thinking to myself almost as much as asking the Lord and therefore did not expect an immediate answer. The service had gone slightly longer than usual, and when I turned on the car radio to the Christian station, an unfamiliar voice was preaching on the air. I didn't normally hear the radio that late and had no idea what would be on the air at that time. No sooner had I turned on the radio than I heard a man shout, "And don't you ladies be cutting your hair. You *know* what the Scriptures say about that!"

Startled, I gave a slight jump in the driver's seat and flipped the knob to turn the radio off. I drove the rest of the way home in silence, partly dumbfounded at the timing that I could not believe was coincidence and partly chuckling at the sense of humor the Lord must have at thinking of ways to deal with us humans. I have never heard any mention of hair on the radio before or since that night. It only reinforced what I had already read in the Word of God. Scissors never touched my hair again.

One Saturday afternoon, I was getting ready to go shopping with Bob. He was eyeing me up and down. Finally he said, "Just how long is your hair going to get?"

"I don't know," I answered him as I smiled.

"Can't you put on your jeans for me?" he asked. "I like you in jeans."

"I know you do. So does every other man in the mall. That's the point."

"I wish you would put on just a little makeup."

"Actually, Bob, I don't feel a bit plain. I feel prettier than ever," I said as I beamed at him and gently twirled in my flowing skirt.

He wasn't ready to agree with me, but I'm not sure that he disagreed either. At least he didn't argue.

Shopping was a new experience and became a vehicle of testimony to the Lord's goodness. The salesclerk would helpfully bring clothes for me to try on or direct me to her own choices.

"How about this one?" the clerk asked as she held up a dress.

"No, that one's too low in the front."

"Oh," she muttered. Pushing through the rack, she pulled out another dress. This one came up to the neck. "Here's a pretty one. These colors will look nice on you too."

"No thanks. I like them to cover my knees."

"Oh," she responded. Diligently searching the rack, she triumphantly pulled another dress and held it up for my inspection.

"No. I prefer to have sleeves that cover my upper arm. I'm in church a lot, and I want to feel comfortable raising my arms to praise the Lord."

"Oh." The clerk stood there for a minute and looked at me before asking, "It must be hard for you to dress like that. How do you do it?"

"On the contrary, it's not hard at all! It's a privilege and a joy. The Lord has done so much for me. He turned my life around, He helps me every day with my husband, my children, and everything that I need, so I count it all joy to dress in a manner that pleases Him. It's the least I can do for the One who gave His life for me. There is a hymn that I love and it expresses the way I look at it. Listen to the words: 'Turn your eyes upon Jesus, look full in His wonderful face, and the things of this earth will grow strangely dim in the light of His glory and grace.' You see, it's simple. Just look at Jesus and fall in love with Him. You will do anything to please the one you love."

In speaking from my heart, I had forgotten where I was. Tears were streaming down my uplifted face as I talked about my Lord. When I looked back at the clerk, she was staring at me with her mouth partly open. We were standing at the front of the store where many people were passing by in the mall. A couple of ladies with their children had seen my expressive discourse and had stopped to listen. As I dug in my purse for a Kleenex to wipe my eyes, the ladies continued their walk down the mall, obviously conversing with each other about what they had just seen and heard. The clerk was still watching me, so I pulled a small tract out of my purse and handed it to her. I showed her the stamp on the back that gave the name and address of the church and thanked her for her service before I left.

Bob might have tried to argue about my outward appearance, but he could not contend with the evident joy that filled my spirit. For six months, he just watched me. I didn't push or argue. I kept sending up prayers and waiting on the Lord to do the work in my husband.

Why am I always surprised when the Lord does answer prayer? When it comes to my husband, I know the answer. It's because Bob doesn't give clues. He thinks privately and then makes announcements that astonish me. "I'm going to the Pearland church with you this Sunday, Mary."

"You are?" I said with glee. "Are you coming to the night service?"

"Oh no. I'll go to the morning service."

I don't know why he thought the morning service was different from the night service. I had been going with him to the other church on Sunday mornings. I didn't even know what the morning services were like at Pearland Tabernacle.

Jennifer and I were thrilled to have Bob and Jeffery with us in Pearland. Brother Barnett vigorously shook Bob's hand and warmly welcomed him. Once we were seated, Bob crossed his arms and proceeded to watch every person and every move. The first visit didn't scare him away. Bob was as much impressed by the preaching of the Word as I was, and he became a Sunday morning regular at the Pentecostal church.

Another six months passed before Bob's next astonishing statement. He had been sitting on the pew every Sunday morning with his arms still crossed but taking in the preaching. Unknown to me, Bob had listened to certain things regarding holiness and decided that he was not good enough to receive the Holy Ghost. He smoked cigarettes, and he thought he had to quit smoking before the Lord would fill him with His Spirit. An evangelist named Brother Bell came in and shed some light on holiness for Bob. Brother Bell said, "You can't clean a fish until you catch him, and some of you will go to the grave with your faults or sins because you try to clean yourself instead of coming to the Lord and letting Him clean you up."

The Lord knew how to reach Bob when I didn't know how. Bob told me later that he spent the following week in prayers of repentance getting himself ready for the next Sunday's service. The following Sunday, Bob walked up to the front after the preaching. Some men gathered around him as he lifted his hands upward. I knelt at the altar bench and prayed fervently. Within minutes, I felt the presence of the Lord move powerfully through me. I began to speak in tongues as the Spirit gave the utterance. One of the men came over and took my hand. He said, "Come with me. I want you to see this."

I followed him to the group of men, and he led me around the circle until I was in front of Bob. I climbed up the steps in front of the altar to be able to see more clearly. Bob's head was back, his hands were high in the air, and he was fluidly speaking in another tongue.

To see my cool, calm, and collected husband so yielded to the Lord was more than I could contain. I fell in a heap on the top step and thanked the Lord profusely. That same man who had come to get me, came to me again. "Sister, get up. Come see your husband."

He gently lifted my hand to help me up and directed me toward Bob. I tumbled into Bob's open arms, and he held me while I clung to his neck and cried on his shoulder until I ran out of tears.

Bob was baptized in Jesus' name that night. We went home holding hands and smiling from ear to ear. "Hey, wipe that smile off your face," I teased him.

"I can't," he said. "I think it may become a fixation."

Jennifer and I laughed. We knew exactly what he meant.

On Monday afternoon, my phone rang. It was Bob. "I went to the mall at lunch time," he informed me. "I must have a new set of eyes or something. Everything looked different to me today. I looked at all of the people in the mall. Everyone's trying to look sexy, but do you know what I thought? They don't look sexy; they have just lost their dignity."

I marveled at his words. I had never thought about it that way before. How true it was: old women trying to look like teenagers, young girls trying to look like women, and teenagers trying to attract attention through sex, hoping for love and settling for lust.

My husband began to change. Through prayer he conquered smoking over a period of three months. He began to dress modestly as a man, putting away his walking shorts and wearing slacks. He put on a shirt when working in the yard.

Another radical change was the decision concerning the television. When we arrived home after a Sunday-night sermon, Bob pulled the plug on all three television sets. "These are leaving the house," he announced.

Jennifer and Jeff spoke simultaneously, "What will we do?"

"Do?" Bob repeated. "You will read. You will play games with each other. You will play outside. You will do your homework. That's what you will do."

And that's what they did. We have never regretted it and never changed it back. It has been a better life than what we had before.

Once Bob received the Holy Ghost, our whole family became part of Pearland Tabernacle. We went to every service together three times a week and anytime something was scheduled in between. Bob was praying at the altar one night and I overheard him. He was saying to the Lord, "She's my love. She's my love."

I had to cry again. Burying my face in my hands, I told Jesus, "I gave it all up for You, and You gave it all back to me. I searched for love all of my life, and when I couldn't find it, I found You. Now, You have filled me with Your Spirit and given me my husband's love too. You have filled Jennifer with Your Spirit and Bob with Your Spirit. You have brought our family close together and bound us with cords of love that cannot be broken. You have done exceedingly and abundantly above and beyond what I could ask or think. You are the God of the impossible. Blessed be the name of the Lord."

Chapter Nineteen

Miracles

Dwayne moved back in with us during his senior year in high school, and Keven spent summer months and holidays with us. Bob and I knew that we could not push and shove holiness or doctrine on boys who were almost grown. We welcomed them home whenever they could be there and we lived a life of holiness in front of them. We let our lives do most of the talking, and the Lord did the rest.

Dwayne was baptized in Jesus' name after he graduated from high school. He went to college in central Texas and came home for visits. He was home for Christmas during his sophomore year when we went to some revival services at Life Tabernacle. The last night of Dwayne's visit, he was filled with the Holy Ghost. He went back to college reading I Corinthians chapter fourteen to his classmates to tell them about the Holy Ghost. Dwayne is now out of college and married to a beautiful Pentecostal girl, Joy Suggett, who is the daughter of a Pentecostal preacher.

Jeffery was baptized in Jesus' name at the age of eight. He was filled with the Holy Ghost at a Texas youth camp when he was twelve. Jeff is now fifteen years old, a freshman in high school, and on the Bible quiz team.

Keven was baptized in Jesus' name before catching a plane to fly back to Washington at the end of a summer he spent with us. In his junior year of college, Keven was back for another visit. He attended every church service with us, and before he left, he was wonderfully filled with the Holy Ghost. Keven is now engaged to a young lady, Shelli Cox, who also has a wonderful heritage in Pentecost.

Sister Gurley came up to me and said, "It has been a long time since I have seen an entire family, including half-grown children, come into the church and every single one of them get baptized in Jesus' name and filled with the Holy Ghost."

Jennifer finished her growing years with the young people in Pearland Tabernacle. She married Conlen Jones, a young man who is sixth-generation Pentecostal and the son of praying parents. He is an answer to my prayers for Jennifer.

Our four children will not need to go through divorces and false doctrine and searching for truth, for peace, and for God. We have a new bloodline: it's the blood of Jesus. Bob and I are watching the blessings of God be poured out upon our children, because His blessings are from generation to generation. I am shouting "Hallelujah!" right now as I write to tell of the great things that He has done. How can I say thank You, Lord? I can tell of Your marvelous works to the children of men.

Brother and Sister Barnett have retired from full-time

pastorship and remain faithful leaders in Pearland Tabernacle. The torch was passed to their son-in-law and daughter, Brother and Sister Gurley. Pearland Tabernacle is blessed—pressed down, shaken together, and running over—with a pastor who preaches the pure Word of God and upholds the beauty of holiness in the midst of a wicked and perverse generation. The clincher is that Pastor and Sister Gurley go deeper than preaching it; they live it.

The Lord allowed me the privilege of working in the church office for over four years, three under Brother Barnett and the rest under Brother Gurley. During that last year, I was planning Jennifer's wedding and we were having a house built. As the stressful year wore on, a terrible pain began to gnaw in my neck and shoulders. I had enjoyed excellent health and energy since receiving the Holy Ghost, except for occasional spinal adjustments needed due to my curved spine. The years of back pain and malaise were only a memory, and I did not welcome an onslaught of pain returning in my body.

The pain intensified until the muscles in my neck and shoulders were daily in spasms. Instead of merely needing occasional adjustments, my spine was going out of alignment every day. No amount of treatments or adjustments by the chiropractor would hold it in place. Each attempt to strengthen the spinal column through exercises was foiled as the pain in my neck and back drew the muscles into racking spasms, pulling the vertebrae out repeatedly.

Forsaking the chiropractor, I tried the family doctor. He took X-rays and together we looked at my curved lower spine and reverse curve in the neck.

"Mary, does your husband beat you?" the doctor asked me.

"No! He does not. You don't know my husband. He's wonderful."

"I'm just looking at your spine," he responded. "Something has hit you and hit you hard. I can only give you pain pills and muscle relaxers."

I took the medications for about three months. Pain sent me back to the doctor. This time he said, "Mary, are you depressed?"

Oh no! I thought. Not that road again. I've been down that path before and I am not going on it again. Then I said to him, "No, sir, I am not depressed. I am in pain."

"I can't help you. You will need to see an orthopedic specialist for traction and therapy."

I went home and prayed, "Lord, please direct me to a doctor. I will only give it one shot. I'm not going through a string of doctors as I did years ago."

A lady who works in the office where Jeffery goes to school told me about a doctor who diagnosed a particular problem for her. I went to see Doctor M and took my spinal X-rays with me. After the usual medical history, she looked at my X-ray films.

"Come here, Mary. Look at this tiny white area between the cervical vertebrae."

"What is it?" I asked her.

"It's a bone spur."

"What does that mean? Why is it there?"

Dr. M stood in front of me and put her hands on my rib cage. "Breath deeply and exhale."

As I breathed in and out, Dr. M watched the degree of expansion in the rib area. "Again," she ordered.

On the next inhalation, she said, "Can you see how little your ribs expand, Mary? Do you ever experience shortness of breath or light-headedness?"

"Yes, I've had trouble with those things for years. What does it mean?"

"Sit down and let's talk," said Dr. M. "You have a type of arthritis called ankylosing spondolitis."

"Anky what?"

Dr. M repeated the term and explained it further. "This type of arthritis affects the ligaments that are attached to the bones. Another name for it is attachment arthritis. It is also called poker spine, because in severe cases, the spinal column becomes fused into one long bony line that makes movement very stiff and difficult or even impossible. There are many ligaments in the lower back and along the spine where the ribs attach. That is why your breathing is hindered and your lower back is painful and weak."

A light bulb came on in my mind as I thought on my symptoms over the past eighteen years of my life. "Dr. M, would this cause weakness and tiredness all over, as in exhaustion?"

"Of course it would. You are not getting a good flow of oxygen, and the pain of arthritis from your neck to your waist is enough to wear anyone out."

I sat on the edge of my chair. "Dr. M, this is very important to me.

"This explains what knocked me down in bed seven years ago. Why couldn't the doctors find it back then? They kept treating me for depression."

"This type of arthritis does not show up in the sediment test in the blood as do other types of arthritis. You are a classic example of what happens to people with spondolitis. It begins to manifest in the early twenties with pain in the ligaments, but it takes years before the bone spurs are formed enough to see them on an X-ray. Many cases are not diagnosed until they reach their early forties, just like you. Here is a book for you to read about it to help you understand it better."

"What will you do for it, Dr. M?"

"I will put you on powerful arthritis medication to allay the inflammation and prescribe a muscle relaxer to stop the spasms in your neck. I advise you to gently exercise your neck every day and move as much as possible to deter the spur formation and bone fusion."

What a relief it was to go home and tell my husband that I was not crazy and the pain and weakness were not just a figment of my imagination or some morbid appeal for attention. It was real, and it had a name.

A visiting minister, Brother Bismark, preached from the beautiful verse of Scripture that states: "Wherefore God also hath highly exalted him [Jesus], and given him a name which is above every name" (Philippians 2:9). He went on to say that if something had a name, it had to bow to the name above every name, the name of Jesus.

Through Dr. M, I had a name for the pain, and I remembered the preaching of the Word of God through Brother Bismark. I took the prescribed medication and began to pray, "Lord Jesus, Your name is above the name of spondolitis, and this affliction must bow to Your glorious and wonderful name."

I was in a lot of pain, but it was so much easier to cope with, because there was now a name and a reason for it. My life needed rearranging, however, to alleviate stress. My pastor and his wife spent several hours talking with me and seeking God's will for my life.

It was obvious that Brother Gurley heard from the Lord because his face showed surprise when he told me that the Lord was bringing in a new church secretary. "Sister Ellis, the Lord is good. He doesn't subtract; He adds and multiplies. The Lord is moving you into a new direction. You have done a fine job as secretary, but there is something else for you now. From working with you in the office, I have seen your ability to write. It comes from God, and we will see what He will do with it."

Six months passed before the Lord brought in the new secretary, but when He did, He brought a jewel. I worked for another six months to train and help young Sister Monceaux. She and her husband, who is assistant pastor to Brother Gurley, make a great team and are a blessing to Pearland Tabernacle.

There is plenty of work to do from home: saints to encourage, new converts to teach, home Bible studies to give, time to spend in prayer and study, and manuscripts to write! But the Lord goes above and beyond what we can ask or think.

My back was going out of alignment daily. Three trips per week to the chiropractor were of no avail. Bob and Dwayne became adept at getting specific spots of my spine back in place between visits to the doctor. I do not advise that for others, but I had been through chiropractic care for eighteen years, and I knew the risks involved. The pain caused when the vertebrae were out of place made me willing to take the risk.

Amid the changes and resurgence of affliction in my life, Sister Nona Freeman's books taught me to praise the Lord and to remember to thank Him in *all* things. Praise and worship lifted my spirit when I began to sag.

The Lord encouraged me through His Word with these verses:

"Be of good courage, and he shall strengthen your heart, all ye that hope in the LORD" (Psalm 31:24).

"The spirit of a man will sustain his infirmity; but a wounded spirit who can bear?" (Proverbs 18:14).

I knew the importance of not becoming discouraged but to keep my eyes lifted upward to the Lord. He would keep my spirit lifted up so that I could bear whatever circumstances I found myself to be in. What a blessing it is to know the Lord!

On Saturday, July 11, 1992, I had taken three prescription-strength tablets of arthritis medication. The pain was so intense that my husband still had to apply a deep-acting muscle cream to my spine. On Sunday morning, our family went to church, as was our custom. Another series of revival services was in progress. The presence of the Lord was powerful among us, and many were going to the altar for prayer. I had been prayed for numerous times, and that morning I wasn't thinking of going to the altar for myself. I was at Jennifer's side and praying for her. My friend Sister Bonnie came and took me by the hand.

"Come on, Sister Mary, this is your day. You are going up front for prayer."

Jennifer joined in with Bonnie, and my husband showed up too. We went to the front and lifted our hands in prayer to the Lord. After a few minutes in prayer I heard Brother Gurley's voice, and hands were laid on my forehead. I was anointed with oil by Brother Gurley and Brother Poe, the evangelist. When they left to pray for the next person, I heard my husband say, "The Lord has done it! You are healed!"

My husband had the Holy Ghost for eight years by that time, and I had only heard him make statements like that in three instances. All three came to pass exactly as he stated through the Holy Ghost. I had no reason, therefore, to doubt what he said. Bob went on to tell me that the symptoms might persist for a while, but the healing had taken place. It was only a matter of time until it would be manifested.

"I believe it!" I said as I looked at him.

From that day to this, my spine has stayed in place. I have not taken one visit to the chiropractor and have no need to go. I have not had any prescription-strength medication for my back and have taken only an occasional over-the-counter tablet of ibuprofen for minor pain when I am under stress. O, taste and see that the Lord is good!

There is one more miracle I must share before closing. After seven years of prayer, intercession, and witnessing, my sister Phyllis is now baptized in Jesus' name and filled with the Holy Ghost. She faithfully attends Life Tabernacle in Houston, and Brother and Sister Kilgore have so graciously ministered to her personally. Together, Phyllis and I cannot praise the Lord enough for His wonderful works to the children of men.